Following the Money:
A Journey Through Shadow Banking and Power Games

Compliance Cowboys: The High-Risk, High-Reward World of 'Ozark'

*by **Slava Solodkiy***

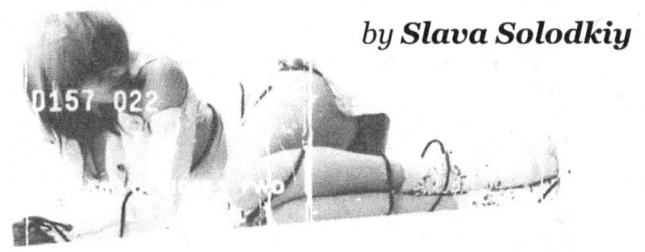

Who Is This Guy, Really?

So, you're about to dive into a book about compliance, fintech, and all the thrilling topics that make most people's eyes glaze over at dinner parties. You're probably thinking, "Who is this Slava Solodkiy fellow, and why should I spend my precious time reading what he has to say?" Fair enough. In an industry bursting at the seams with self-proclaimed gurus and influencers who "teach sex and give advice without ever having tried it themselves," I'm the guy who's not only been there and done that but has also ventured into all the shadiest corners to try everything firsthand.

Yes, that's right—I didn't just read the manual; I helped write it, footnotes and all, after stress-testing every rule in the book. While others were busy pontificating from the safety of their ergonomic chairs, I was in the trenches, building a crypto-friendly digital bank from scratch. Because, you know, starting with something simple just isn't my style. Securing a U.S. banking license? Why not add that to the to-do list. Attracting clients from 26 countries without spending a single dollar on marketing? Sure, let's make it interesting.

Over the past decade, I've founded and led two fintech startups, invested in five digital banks, and somehow convinced people to let me build a regulated, crypto-friendly bank without immediately calling security. My journey has taken me through the wild west of high-risk banking, the rollercoaster of crypto innovation, and the labyrinthine world of AML compliance. I've seen things that would make a compliance officer wake up in a cold sweat.

People seem to enjoy inviting me to speak at events like Money2020 and the Singapore Fintech Festival—perhaps they appreciate a good cautionary tale. I've even had the audacity to lecture at places like Wharton and INSEAD, which still surprises my old professors to this day. I've penned a few things along the way, including "The First Fintech Bank's Arrival" and the annual fintech research "Money of the Future." Apparently, some folks find my insights valuable—or they just enjoy watching someone navigate the compliance minefield with the grace of a caffeinated squirrel.

But let's get down to brass tacks: why should you read this book? Because in a world where so many are eager to dish out advice without ever getting their hands dirty, I've been knee-deep in the muck, making mistakes so you don't have to. I bring stories from the front lines of fintech and compliance, sprinkled with a healthy dose of self-irony and a dash of sarcasm.

Think of this book as a behind-the-scenes tour of the fintech world, guided by someone who's not afraid to admit that sometimes the best lessons come from the worst decisions. You'll get the unvarnished truth about what it's like to build a bank from the ground up, wrestle with regulators, and try to innovate in an industry that often prefers the status quo.

So grab a cup of coffee—or something stronger if you're feeling particularly adventurous—and join me as we navigate the exhilarating, infuriating, and occasionally rewarding world of high-risk banking and compliance. At the very least, you'll get a few laughs and maybe even learn something that the so-called gurus won't tell you—mostly because they haven't experienced it themselves.

Welcome to my world. It's messy, unpredictable, and definitely not for the faint of heart. But if you're up for the ride, I promise it'll be worth your time. In addition to my misadventures, I'm an LP at Balaji's fund (and AAL.VC). I also host the "*Follow The Money [Anti] Money Laundering Show*" podcast, where we delve into the riveting realms of Compliance, KYC, EDD, AML, GovTech, digital identity, network states and metastates, chartered cities, and new unions. If that doesn't get your heart racing, well, you're probably normal.

Introduction: High-Risk vs. Shadow Banking—The Good, the Bad, and the Downright Sketchy

Picture this: two banks walk into a bar. One is labeled "High-Risk Banking," the other "Shadow Banking." They look similar, dress the same, and both order the top-shelf whiskey. But while one is busy checking IDs and paying taxes, the other slips something under the table and exits through the back door. Welcome to the nuanced world of high-risk and shadow banking.

High-risk banking is like running a legitimate business in a rough neighborhood. You're dealing with clients that mainstream banks avoid—think cannabis startups, cryptocurrency exchanges, and fintech innovators. It's not that these clients are inherently bad; they're just... misunderstood.

At ArivalBank.com, we saw high-risk banking as the frontier of financial services. Sure, the terrain was rocky, and the stakes were high, but with the right compliance [Compliance Demystified: A Beginner's Guide[1]] measures, it was not only manageable but also rewarding. We built our processes like a fortress, with compliance as the impenetrable walls keeping out the barbarians at the gate. Our high-risk clients appreciated the honesty. They weren't looking to skirt the law; they just needed a bank that understood their unique challenges and was willing to provide support without judgmental glances or exorbitant fees.

Shadow Banking: The Financial World's Speakeasy

On the flip side, shadow banking operates in the... well, shadows. It's the speakeasy of finance—unregulated, often unlicensed, and catering to those who prefer anonymity over accountability.

---

[1] https://medium.com/@slavasolodkiy_67243/compliance-demystified-a-beginners-guide-d41342fdc056

Shadow banking entities might offer services similar to traditional banks but without the pesky oversight. Need a quick loan with no questions asked? They've got you covered. Want to move large sums across borders without attracting attention? Step right up.

But here's the catch: shadow banking plays a significant role in financial instability. Remember the 2008 financial crisis? Shadow banking was the life of that ill-fated party.

Wirecard: When Shadows Masquerade as Light

Take **Wirecard**, for example. Once hailed as a fintech darling in Germany, it turned out to be more illusion than innovation. With complex structures and phantom profits, Wirecard showcased how shadow banking can operate under the veneer of legitimacy.

They didn't just bend the rules; they performed a full-on gymnastics routine around them. Offshore accounts, suspicious transactions, and a reluctance to answer simple questions like "Where's the money?" eventually led to their downfall. It's a cautionary tale of what happens when transparency is sacrificed on the altar of rapid growth.

ENRC: Mining Riches and Digging Holes

Then there's the case of the **Eurasian Natural Resources Corporation (ENRC)**. Operating in high-risk regions with even higher-risk practices, ENRC [From Arival to ENRC: A Pattern of Behavior? Or Just a Coincidence?[2]] became a poster child for how not to manage compliance and face of Kleptopia[3].

Allegations of corruption, fraud, and human rights abuses swirled around them like a tornado, but they seemed unperturbed, continuing operations with the confidence of a gambler on a hot

---

[2] https://medium.com/@slavasolodkiy_67243/from-enrc-to-arival-a-pattern-of-behavior-or-just-a-coincidence-b96f30e1b3f8

[3] https://amzn.to/4hLfKDl

streak. Their use of shadow financial channels to move money under the radar exemplified the perils of unregulated finance.

The Fine Line Between Innovation and Exploitation

High-risk banking walks a tightrope. On one side lies the opportunity to serve underserved markets and drive innovation. On the other, the abyss of regulatory non-compliance [Compliance is sexy, and Arival knows it[4]] and ethical lapses.

At ArivalBank.com, we chose to walk that line with our eyes wide open, armed with robust compliance frameworks and a commitment to transparency. We believed that you could embrace innovation without compromising on integrity. Shadow banking, in contrast, often leaps off the tightrope, trusting that the pile of ill-gotten gains will cushion the fall.

Why High-Risk Doesn't Have to Mean High Reward for Criminals

By implementing stringent compliance measures, high-risk banks can prevent becoming unwitting accomplices to financial crimes. This includes:

- **Enhanced Due Diligence**: Going beyond the basics to truly understand who you're dealing with.
- **Transaction Monitoring**: Keeping an eagle eye on the flow of funds.
- **Regulatory Collaboration**: Working with, not against, regulators to ensure best practices.

It's like running a nightclub in a tough part of town. You can let in the edgy crowd without turning a blind eye to illegal activities. Good music, good vibes, and a zero-tolerance policy for troublemakers.

---

[4] https://medium.com/arivalbank/compliance-is-sexy-and-arival-knows-it-3d7094f53131

Shedding Light on the Shadows

The world doesn't need more shadow banks—it needs institutions willing to tackle high-risk markets with integrity and transparency. By distinguishing ourselves from the murky practices of shadow banking, we aimed to set a new standard.

So, the next time someone confuses high-risk banking with shadow banking, feel free to enlighten them. One operates within the framework of law, pushing boundaries responsibly. The other skirts the edges, exploiting loopholes until they become sinkholes.

In the grand scheme of finance, it's better to be the lighthouse guiding ships safely to shore than the siren luring them onto the rocks.

Part I. **Abnormal is the New Normal: A Journey Through High-Risk Banking and Compliance**

Chapter 1: Compliance Is the New Black

Once upon a time, the word "compliance" was enough to induce yawns at board meetings. It conjured images of drab cubicles, endless paperwork, and bureaucrats wielding rubber stamps like scepters of tedium. Compliance was the necessary evil, the party pooper reminding everyone that fun had limits set by law.

But somewhere between the corporate scandals, the digital revolution, and the globalization of, well, everything, compliance got interesting. Scratch that—it became essential, even sexy. In today's high-stakes financial world, compliance isn't just the rulebook; it's the playbook. It's the unsung hero keeping the global economy from teetering off a cliff.

Consider this: Every morning, you wake up and check your smartphone (after unlocking it with your fingerprint—thanks, biometric compliance). You might transfer money via a digital bank, invest in cryptocurrency, or donate to a crowdfunding campaign. Each of these actions is steeped in layers of compliance protocols designed to protect you and the financial system from nefarious actors.

So how did we get here? How did compliance transform from the dull uncle at the family reunion to the cool cousin with the insider scoop?

From Back Office to Center Stage

Rewind to the early 2000s. The financial world was rocked by scandals that made the Wild West look orderly. Enron, WorldCom, and a slew of others imploded under the weight of their deceit.

Regulatory bodies responded with a vengeance, rolling out laws like Sarbanes-Oxley that demanded greater transparency and accountability.

Compliance departments grew overnight, not out of passion but out of sheer necessity. Companies hired armies of lawyers and auditors, turning compliance into a growth industry. Yet, it was still seen as a cost center—a grudge purchase akin to insurance.

Then came the digital tsunami.

The rise of fintech, cryptocurrencies, and global e-commerce shattered traditional financial models. Money started moving at the speed of light across borders, through channels regulators hadn't even dreamed of. Cybercriminals and money launderers rejoiced; everyone else panicked.

Suddenly, compliance wasn't just about ticking boxes—it was about survival.

Compliance as Competitive Edge

When we founded **ArivalBank.com**, a digital bank born in the cloud era, we faced a choice. We could treat compliance as a burdensome obligation, or we could turn it into our secret weapon. We chose the latter.

Imagine pitching to a room full of fintech startups, crypto exchanges, and cross-border e-commerce platforms—all of them underserved by traditional banks scared stiff of anything that doesn't fit their mold. We told them, "Not only will we bank you, but we'll protect you with a compliance framework so advanced, it makes Fort Knox look like a piggy bank."

That got their attention.

By leveraging cutting-edge technologies—think AI-driven KYC (Know Your Customer) processes, machine learning algorithms for transaction monitoring, and real-time AML (Anti-Money

Laundering) analytics—we turned compliance into a selling point. Clients didn't just choose us because we were willing to bank them; they chose us because we could safeguard them in a volatile financial landscape.

The Global Village of Complexity

Globalization has turned the world into a village—a village with over 190 sets of laws, regulations, and languages. Navigating this maze is a herculean task. Every cross-border transaction is a potential minefield of compliance issues: sanctions, tax laws, reporting requirements, you name it.

But where others saw complexity, we saw opportunity.

By mastering the art of global compliance, we became the go-to guides for businesses venturing into new markets. We helped them avoid the pitfalls that come with international expansion, turning compliance into a bridge rather than a barrier.

Democratizing Compliance

Here's a plot twist: Compliance isn't just for the big players anymore. In the age of the gig economy, digital nomads, and micro-entrepreneurs, compliance touches everyone.

Take, for instance, the freelance graphic designer in Berlin working for clients in San Francisco and Tokyo. She's subject to data protection laws like GDPR, tax regulations across three countries, and payment processing rules that would make anyone's head spin.

The democratization of compliance means that individuals and small businesses need solutions just as robust as those of multinational corporations. This opens the door for innovation— streamlined compliance apps, user-friendly legal platforms, and services that make navigating regulations as easy as ordering a latte.

Scandals as Catalysts

Nothing accelerates the evolution of compliance like a good scandal. When **Wirecard** [Money Men[5]] collapsed, it wasn't just a corporate failure; it was a systemic one. Billions evaporated, regulatory bodies were caught flat-footed, and trust in the financial system took another hit. Similar stories played out with **FTX**, **Tether**, and other high-profile cases.

Each scandal served as a wake-up call, highlighting the dire consequences of lax compliance. But they also underscored an important point: Robust compliance isn't just about avoiding penalties; it's about building trust.

At Arival, we didn't hide our compliance measures behind legalese and fine print. We put them front and center. Transparency became part of our brand identity. Clients knew exactly how we protected them and their assets, fostering a level of trust that marketing dollars can't buy.

Innovation Meets Regulation

You might think compliance stifles innovation. On the contrary, it can be a catalyst. When we developed the **Navalny Card** project back in 2012, the idea was radical: create an AML-first digital banking app and card that could support political activists while adhering to strict compliance standards. It was a tightrope walk between innovation and regulation, but it proved that the two could coexist—even thrive together.

Similarly, our work on **Nansen.ID** aimed to rethink digital identity [[Digital] Identity is the new money[6]] verification, taking inspiration from the Nansen Passport used during the interwar period to aid stateless refugees. By leveraging blockchain technology and advanced biometrics, we envisioned a digital identity solution that could

---

[5] https://amzn.to/3YxUfNt

[6] https://www.slideshare.net/slideshow/digital-identity-is-the-new-money/100705902

withstand the rigors of modern compliance while empowering individuals.

The New Normal

In a world marked by rapid economic shifts, political instability, and technological disruption, the only constant is change—and with it, risk.

Compliance has become the compass guiding institutions through uncharted waters. It's the shield against cyber threats, the map through regulatory jungles, and the handshake that builds trust in virtual spaces.

Banks and financial institutions operating on the fringes—whether by choice or necessity—can't afford to view compliance as an afterthought. It's the foundation upon which sustainable operations are built.

Why Compliance Matters More Than Ever

As we look ahead, the challenges won't get any simpler. The rise of decentralized finance (DeFi), the proliferation of digital assets, and the advent of new technologies like quantum computing will introduce complexities we can't yet fully grasp.

Compliance will be the anchor in these turbulent times.

But perhaps more importantly, compliance is about ethics. It's about doing the right thing, not because regulations demand it, but because it's integral to building a better financial system. One that is inclusive, transparent, and resilient. **Compliance isn't just about following rules—it's about setting standards.**

Chapter 2: The Art of Knowing Your Customer (Without Being a Stalker)

Remember the good old days when banking was simple? You'd stroll into your local branch, greet Susan the teller (who knew your dog's name and your coffee order), deposit a check, and be on your merry way. No fuss, no muss, and certainly no one asking for a DNA sample to prove you weren't laundering money for an international cartel.

Alas, those days are as extinct as Blockbuster Video. Welcome to the era of **KYC** (Know Your Customer) and **AML** (Anti-Money Laundering), where banks need to know not just who you are, but who you've ever been, who you might become, and whether you prefer cats over dogs (because that might be a red flag).

KYC and AML: The Dynamic Duo Fighting Financial Crime

In the superhero universe of finance, KYC and AML are the caped crusaders battling the jokers of money laundering, fraud, and terrorism financing. They're like Batman and Robin, if Batman had to fill out endless paperwork and Robin spent his days analyzing blockchain transactions.

At first glance, KYC and AML might seem about as exciting as watching paint dry. But consider this: global money laundering transactions account for roughly 2–5% of global GDP, or $800 billion to $2 trillion annually. Suddenly, those acronyms become a lot more interesting, don't they?

From Paperwork to Pixels: The Evolution of Verification

In the beginning, verifying a customer's identity was straightforward: check their ID, make sure they're not visibly wearing a ski mask, and you're good to go. But as financial crime became more sophisticated, so did the need for robust verification methods.

Enter **digital identity verification**, the financial world's answer to the bouncer with facial recognition at an exclusive nightclub. Except this bouncer also scans your fingerprints, analyzes your voice patterns, and maybe even checks how you type. Paranoid? Perhaps. Necessary? Absolutely.

At **ArivalBank.com**, we embraced this shift with open arms (and a healthy dose of skepticism). We realized that traditional methods were about as effective as a screen door on a submarine. So, we dove headfirst into biometrics, AI, and blockchain—not just to keep up with the Joneses but to outpace the Sopranos.

Machine Learning: The Crystal Ball of Compliance

Imagine having a crystal ball that could predict which customers might be trouble before they even walk through the (virtual) door. That's the promise of machine learning in KYC and AML. These algorithms sift through mountains of data, spotting patterns that would make a conspiracy theorist blush.

We implemented systems that could flag suspicious activity faster than you can say "offshore account." Transactions to sanctioned countries? Detected. Unusual spikes in account activity? Alerted. Customer's name matches an international fugitive? Well, that's a phone call we'd rather not make.

But here's where it gets tricky. Machines, for all their brilliance, lack nuance. They might flag a perfectly innocent customer because their middle name matches someone on a watchlist. So, we had to balance the cold efficiency of algorithms with the warm judgment of human analysts—a marriage of silicon and carbon that keeps the gears of compliance turning smoothly.

Digital Identity: The New Gold Rush

In a world where deepfakes can mimic anyone's face and voice, proving you are who you say you are has become a Herculean task. Digital identity is the new gold rush, and everyone's scrambling to stake their claim.

We took inspiration from Fridtjof Nansen, a Norwegian explorer who, in the aftermath of World War I, created the "Nansen Passport" for stateless refugees. It was a beacon of hope in a tumultuous world—a way to prove one's identity when all else was lost.

Our modern-day equivalent, **Nansen.ID**, aimed to provide a secure, unforgeable digital identity. Using blockchain (because it's not a tech solution unless blockchain is involved), we crafted a system where your identity isn't just a piece of paper or a database entry—it's an encrypted, tamper-proof digital asset.

AML: Because Crime Doesn't Pay (But It Tries Really Hard)

Anti-Money Laundering efforts are like the unsung janitors of the financial world, cleaning up messes nobody wants to acknowledge exist. They're not glamorous, but without them, the whole system would collapse under the weight of its own corruption.

Our approach to AML was proactive. We didn't wait for the regulators to wag their fingers or for the media to expose a scandal. We built systems that could detect and prevent illicit activities in real-time, much to the chagrin of anyone hoping to sneak a few million through our accounts unnoticed.

We used tools like **OSIT** (Open Source Intelligence Tools) to scour public records, social media, and even the dark web. Yes, we went there—virtually, of course. All in the name of ensuring that our bank didn't become an unwitting accomplice in funding the next big villain's secret lair.

The Ironic Twist of Trust

Here's the irony: in an effort to build trust with our customers, we had to subject them to scrutiny that bordered on intrusive. It's like dating someone who insists on a background check before the first date. Unsettling? Maybe. But in a world where identity theft and financial fraud are rampant, a little due diligence goes a long way.

We recognized that trust is a two-way street. So, we were transparent about our processes, explaining why we needed certain information and how it protected both the customer and the bank. We even injected a bit of humor into our communications— because nothing eases the awkwardness of asking for a selfie with your ID quite like a well-placed joke.

Compliance Doesn't Have to Be a Four-Letter Word

Let's be honest: compliance gets a bad rap. It's seen as the fun police, the red tape, the obstacle to innovation. But what if we flipped the script? What if compliance was the catalyst for innovation?

At ArivalBank.com, we discovered that by embracing the challenges of KYC and AML, we could actually enhance the customer experience. Faster onboarding, fewer false positives, and a stronger security posture all contributed to a smoother, more trustworthy service.

We turned compliance into a competitive advantage. While other banks were bogged down in manual processes and outdated systems, we leveraged technology to stay ahead of the curve. And we did it all while maintaining a sense of humor—because if you can't laugh at the absurdity of filling out your 27th compliance form, what's the point?

The Future Is Compliant (and That's a Good Thing)

As we look toward the future, one thing is clear: compliance isn't going anywhere. If anything, it's becoming more integral to the fabric of finance. And maybe that's not such a bad thing.

In a world where technological advancements can be both a boon and a bane, having robust systems to ensure integrity and trust is essential. KYC, AML, digital identity—they're not just buzzwords or hurdles to clear. They're the pillars supporting a financial ecosystem that's fair, transparent, and resilient.

So, the next time you're asked to provide a bit more information or go through an extra verification step, remember: it's all part of the grand dance of compliance. A dance that keeps the bad actors off the floor and ensures everyone else can enjoy the music.

And who knows? Maybe one day, compliance will be as beloved as your favorite app or as exciting as the latest tech gadget. Okay, maybe that's a stretch. But a banker can dream.

Chapter 3: Walking the Tightrope—What Regulators Really Want

If you thought your in-laws had high expectations, wait until you meet financial regulators. They don't just want you to follow the rules; they expect you to anticipate their dreams, fulfill their unspoken desires, and maybe, just maybe, read their minds. In the high-stakes world of finance, regulators are the omnipresent guardians, the unsmiling sentinels standing between you and the abyss of non-compliance.

But let's be honest—regulators aren't out to ruin your fun (though it might feel that way when you're buried under a mountain of paperwork). They're the necessary chaperones at the wild party of finance, ensuring that everyone behaves, or at least doesn't set the place on fire.

Transparency: The New Black

First on the regulators' wish list is transparency. Think of it as financial nudity—they want to see everything. Every transaction, every client interaction, every suspicious eyebrow raise documented and accessible. It's like being on a reality show where the cameras never stop rolling.

At **ArivalBank.com**, we embraced this with the enthusiasm of a teenager oversharing on social media. We built systems that tracked, recorded, and reported our every move—not because we loved the spotlight, but because transparency builds trust. And in a world where trust is harder to come by than a unicorn in a haystack, that mattered.

Risk Assessment: Channeling Your Inner Psychic

Regulators expect you to not only manage risks but to predict them. Yes, they want you to be the Nostradamus of finance, foreseeing potential vulnerabilities before they materialize. It's a bit like being asked to predict the weather six months from now while blindfolded, but hey, challenge accepted.

We developed robust risk assessment frameworks that evaluated everything from geopolitical shifts to the likelihood of a client suddenly deciding to dabble in international arms dealing. It's all in a day's work when you're trying to stay one step ahead of both criminals and regulators.

CDD: The Fine Art of Not Being Creepy

Knowing your customer is essential, but there's a thin line between due diligence and stalking. Regulators expect you to verify identities, understand financial backgrounds, and assess risks—all without violating privacy laws or triggering restraining orders.

We navigated this tightrope by leveraging technology that could sift through public records, transaction histories, and other data points to build a risk profile. All done with the utmost respect for privacy and a dash of finesse. After all, nothing says "we value you" like not prying into your high school diary entries.

Enhanced Due Diligence: When Regular Scrutiny Just Isn't Enough

For high-risk clients, regulators want you to don your detective hat and dig deeper. Enhanced Due Diligence (EDD) is like the VIP section of compliance—exclusive, more intense, and with a stricter dress code.

At ArivalBank.com, EDD meant going beyond the surface. We analyzed social connections, business interests, and any hint of scandal that might indicate a risk. It's amazing what you can find with a little digging—and sometimes, ignorance is not bliss.

Ongoing Monitoring: The Gift That Keeps on Giving

Compliance isn't a "set it and forget it" endeavor. Regulators expect continuous vigilance, like a security guard who never sleeps (or at least has a very effective caffeine regimen).

Our systems monitored transactions in real-time, flagging anything that deviated from the norm. Unusually large transfers, sudden activity in dormant accounts, transactions with sanctioned countries—we saw it all and acted swiftly. It's like being a lifeguard at the world's busiest pool, always watching for the kid who's about to run on the wet deck.

Culture of Compliance: More Than Just a Motto on a Coffee Mug

Perhaps the most intangible yet critical expectation is fostering a culture of compliance. Regulators want to see that compliance isn't just a department—it's woven into the fabric of the organization. Think of it as company DNA, but with fewer double helices and more ethical guidelines.

We cultivated this culture by making compliance everyone's responsibility. From the CEO to the intern fetching coffee (which, by the way, also had to comply with fair trade regulations), everyone understood the importance of adhering to the rules. Regular training sessions, open communication channels, and a zero-tolerance policy for violations were the pillars of our approach.

Embracing the Dance with Regulators

Navigating regulatory expectations is a bit like dancing with a very strict partner—they lead, you follow, and stepping on toes is highly discouraged. But once you learn the steps, it becomes a collaborative performance.

At ArivalBank.com, we didn't see regulators as adversaries but as partners in maintaining the integrity of the financial system. Sure, they might crash the party occasionally, but their presence keeps the venue from descending into chaos.

The Compliance Compass

Understanding what regulators expect isn't just about avoiding fines or sanctions; it's about building a sustainable, reputable business. Compliance is the compass that keeps you on course amid the turbulent seas of finance.

So, the next time you receive a lengthy memo from a regulatory body, don't groan (too loudly). Instead, see it as a roadmap—a guide to not only meeting expectations but exceeding them. After all, in a world where trust is the most valuable currency, compliance is how you mint it.

Chapter 4: Compliance—Your Secret Weapon in Disguise

Let's face it: Compliance isn't the prom queen of business concepts. It's more like the hall monitor—necessary but rarely adored. Yet, what if I told you that compliance could be your secret weapon, the unsung hero that doesn't just keep you out of jail but propels your business forward? Sounds like a plot twist worthy of a blockbuster movie, doesn't it?

Efficiency: Turning Red Tape into a Red Carpet

First up, compliance can actually make your operations more efficient. Wait, what? Isn't compliance supposed to bog you down with endless forms and procedures?

Not if you play it right.

By implementing robust compliance systems, you automate repetitive tasks, reduce errors, and streamline processes. It's like having a well-oiled machine that purrs along while your competitors are stuck cranking rusty gears.

At **ArivalBank.com**, we found that investing in compliance technology saved us time and money in the long run. Fewer manual checks meant fewer mistakes and happier clients. Who knew that following the rules could be so... liberating?

Trust and Reputation: The Currency You Can't Buy

In a world where scandals erupt faster than you can say "press release," maintaining a sterling reputation is priceless. Clients want to know that their money is safe, that they're dealing with an institution that won't end up on the front page for all the wrong reasons.

Strong compliance is like a badge of honor. It tells the world, "We play by the rules, and we're proud of it." This trust translates into customer loyalty, positive word-of-mouth, and a competitive edge that's hard to beat.

Remember when we talked about Wirecard's fall from grace? Yeah, let's avoid that.

Competitive Differentiation: Standing Out by Standing Up

In saturated markets, differentiation is key. While others might cut corners or view compliance as an afterthought, you can position yourself as the gold standard.

Clients in high-risk sectors are particularly appreciative of banks that take compliance seriously. They're tired of being treated like pariahs and are eager to partner with institutions that offer both services and peace of mind.

By championing compliance, you don't just meet expectations—you exceed them. It's like bringing gourmet appetizers to a potluck where everyone else brought chips.

Innovation and Growth: Compliance as a Catalyst

Believe it or not, compliance can spur innovation. When faced with regulatory challenges, you're forced to think creatively, to develop solutions that not only meet but surpass requirements.

We embraced technologies like AI, blockchain, and machine learning—not just for the cool factor but to enhance our compliance capabilities. This investment didn't just keep regulators happy; it opened doors to new products, services, and markets.

Compliance pushed us to be better, smarter, and more agile. It's the kind of pressure that turns coal into diamonds.

Cost Savings: Pay Now or Pay Much More Later

Yes, compliance requires upfront investment. But consider the alternative—fines, legal fees, reputational damage, and the potential collapse of your business.

It's like choosing between regular car maintenance or waiting until the engine explodes. One costs money; the other costs a fortune (and maybe your eyebrows).

By proactively managing compliance, we avoided costly pitfalls. Think of it as insurance that you actually have control over.

Rewriting the Narrative

It's time to change how we view compliance. Not as a ball and chain, but as a sturdy pair of wings that can elevate your business to new heights.

At ArivalBank.com, compliance wasn't just a department—it was part of our DNA. It informed our decisions, inspired innovation, and built a fortress of trust around our brand.

So, the next time someone groans at the mention of compliance, feel free to enlighten them. Tell them that in the grand chess game of business, compliance is the queen—versatile, powerful, and essential for victory.

Embrace compliance, and you might just find that it's not a burden but a blessing in disguise.

Chapter 5: Compliance-as-a-Service— Renting Your Way to Regulatory Bliss

In the ever-spinning hamster wheel of compliance, innovation isn't just helpful—it's a lifeline. Traditional compliance methods are about as effective in today's world as using a flip phone to navigate a smartphone app. Enter **Compliance-as-a-Service** [Arrival of the compliance-as-a-service[7]] and **Open Source Intelligence Technology (OSIT)**—the dynamic duo ready to drag compliance kicking and screaming into the 21st century.

CaaS: Because Owning Is So Last Century

---

[7] https://www.slideshare.net/slideshow/arrival-of-aid-complianceasaservice-solution/174265982

Remember when owning a car was a status symbol? Now, everyone and their grandmother is using ride-sharing apps. The same shift is happening with compliance. Why build and maintain a colossal compliance department when you can essentially **rent** one?

Compliance-as-a-Service offers institutions access to top-tier compliance solutions without the headache of developing them in-house. It's like subscribing to a streaming service but instead of binge-watching shows, you're binge-complying with regulations.

At **ArivalBank.com**, we embraced CaaS not because we're lazy (well, maybe a little), but because it made sense. It allowed us to stay nimble, adapt quickly to regulatory changes, and access specialized expertise without having to hire an army of compliance officers.

OSIT: Spying for the Greater Good

Open Source Intelligence Technology (OSIT) sounds like something out of a spy thriller, and honestly, it kind of is. OSIT involves collecting and analyzing publicly available information to make informed decisions.

Think of it as using the vast ocean of data out there to your advantage—legally, of course. From social media posts to public records, OSIT tools help institutions uncover hidden risks and stay one step ahead of the bad guys.

We leveraged OSIT at ArivalBank.com to enhance our due diligence processes. It was like having Sherlock Holmes on retainer, minus the opium addiction and violin solos.

Artificial Intelligence and Machine Learning: Robots to the Rescue

If you haven't noticed, AI is everywhere—from recommending your next binge-watch to driving cars (sort of). In compliance, **Artificial**

Intelligence (AI) and **Machine Learning (ML)** are game-changers.

These technologies can process vast amounts of data faster than you can say "regulatory non-compliance." They identify patterns, flag anomalies, and even predict potential risks before they materialize. It's like having a crystal ball that actually works.

By integrating AI and ML into our compliance systems, we transformed from reactive to proactive. Instead of scrambling to address issues after they arose, we could prevent them from happening in the first place. It's the difference between putting out fires and fireproofing your house.

Blockchain: Not Just for Cryptocurrency Anymore

Ah, **Blockchain**—the buzzword that refuses to go away. While often associated with cryptocurrencies and speculative bubbles, blockchain technology has serious applications in compliance.

Blockchain provides a secure, transparent ledger that can enhance data integrity and streamline compliance processes. It's tamper-proof, which means once data is recorded, it can't be altered without leaving a trace. We explored using blockchain at ArivalBank.com to manage KYC data. It offered a way to securely share information with trusted partners without compromising client confidentiality. Plus, saying we used blockchain made us sound cutting-edge at cocktail parties.

Biometrics and Identity Verification: Because Passwords Are So 2010

In an age where deepfakes and identity theft are rampant, traditional verification methods are about as secure as a screen door on a submarine.

Enter **Biometrics**—fingerprints, facial recognition, voice patterns—the unique characteristics that are hard to fake (unless you're Ethan Hunt from Mission: Impossible).

By implementing biometric verification, we enhanced security while improving user experience. Clients appreciated the seamless onboarding, and we appreciated not having to deal with password reset requests every five minutes.

Innovation Isn't Optional—It's Essential

The compliance landscape is like a game of whack-a-mole—the moment you address one issue, another pops up. Innovations like CaaS, OSIT, AI, blockchain, and biometrics aren't just nice-to-haves; they're necessities in staying ahead.

At ArivalBank.com, we recognized that clinging to outdated methods was a recipe for disaster. Embracing innovation allowed us to adapt, evolve, and thrive in a regulatory environment that grows more complex by the day.

The Future Is Now, and It's Compliant

The compliance challenges of tomorrow are already knocking on our door today. By leveraging these cutting-edge technologies and approaches, we don't just keep up with the times—we set the pace.

Innovation and compliance might seem like strange bedfellows, but together, they form a powerful alliance. So here's to thinking outside the box, embracing the new, and making compliance not just a requirement but a cornerstone of success.

Because in the grand scheme of things, it's better to ride the wave of innovation than to be left behind clinging to outdated practices.

Chapter 6: Correspondent Banking—The Complex Dance of Global Finance

If international finance were a grand ballroom, **correspondent banking** [Correspondent banking market overview[8]] would be the intricate choreography that keeps everyone from waltzing into each other's toes. It's the elegant yet complex dance that allows money to glide across borders, currencies, and regulations with (ideally) seamless grace. But as with any elaborate performance, one misstep can lead to a cascade of chaos—or at least a few stubbed toes.

The Invisible Web We All Rely On

At its core, correspondent banking [Fintech no more: correspondent banking is still an untouched niche[9]] is a simple concept: **Bank A** in one country holds an account with **Bank B** in another country. This relationship allows customers of Bank A to make international transactions as if they were locals in Bank B's country. It's like having a friend with VIP access who can get you into the exclusive clubs abroad—no questions asked.

This system is the unsung hero of international trade, remittances, and cross-border investments. Without it, sending money abroad would involve stuffing cash into a bottle and hoping the ocean currents are in your favor. It's the backstage crew that keeps the show running while the stars (read: big banks) bask in the spotlight.

Compliance Nightmares: A Global Game of Whac-A-Mole

But with great power comes great responsibility—and a mountain of compliance challenges. Navigating the labyrinth of international

---

[8] https://www.slideshare.net/slideshow/correspondent-banking-market-overview/262636406

[9] https://www.linkedin.com/pulse/fintech-more-correspondent-banking-still-untouched-niche-solodkiy/

regulations is about as straightforward as solving a Rubik's Cube blindfolded while riding a unicycle.

Every country has its own rules, and they don't always play nice together. **Anti-Money Laundering (AML)**, **Counter-Terrorist Financing (CTF)**, sanctions lists, **Know Your Customer's Customer (KYCC)**—it's an alphabet soup of potential pitfalls. One slip-up, and you might find yourself entangled in legal woes that make Dante's Inferno look like a leisurely stroll.

Just ask any bank that's faced multi-billion-dollar fines for compliance failures. It's enough to give even the most seasoned banker insomnia—or at least a chronic eye twitch.

KYCC: Knowing Your Customer Isn't Enough

In correspondent banking, it's not sufficient to know your customer—you need to know who your customer's customers are. It's the financial equivalent of meeting your significant other's entire extended family, including that twice-removed cousin with the dubious side business.

KYCC requires a deep dive into the operations of your respondent banks. Who are they dealing with? Are they following robust compliance protocols? Do they have clients on sanctioned lists? It's a game of financial detective that would make Sherlock Holmes raise an eyebrow.

At ArivalBank.com, we approached KYCC like investigative journalists—minus the press badges and questionable trench coats. We needed to ensure that our network didn't become a conduit for illicit activities. It's a daunting task, but the alternative is worse—becoming the unwitting getaway driver in a global heist.

Technology to the Rescue: The Digital Swiss Army Knife

Thankfully, we're not navigating this minefield with paper maps and compasses. Advanced technologies like **AI** and **machine**

learning have become indispensable tools in managing correspondent banking compliance.

These systems can analyze vast amounts of data in real-time, flagging suspicious transactions faster than a caffeinated cheetah. They help us spot patterns that might indicate money laundering, fraud, or other nefarious activities—it's like having a vigilant first mate who never sleeps.

Blockchain technology also holds promise, offering immutable records that enhance transparency and trust. Imagine a world where every transaction is a verified entry in a ledger that can't be altered—a compliance officer's dream and a fraudster's nightmare.

The Human Element: Can't Live Without It

Despite technological advancements, the human element remains crucial. Judgment calls, ethical considerations, and nuanced understanding of geopolitical risks can't be fully outsourced to algorithms—at least not until robots develop a conscience (and that's a sci-fi plot we're not ready to tackle).

Training teams to understand the complexities of international regulations is essential. It's like teaching everyone to be polyglot diplomats fluent in legalese, financial jargon, and the subtle art of reading between the lines.

Cracks in the Foundation: When the System Falters

Despite its critical role, correspondent banking is facing a slew of problems that would give even the most stoic economist a case of the jitters. High costs, slow transaction times, and a lack of transparency are just the tip of the iceberg.

For businesses and individuals in developing countries, these issues aren't just inconvenient—they're debilitating. Imagine trying to run a business when paying a supplier in another country is as time-consuming and costly as sending goods via carrier pigeon.

The Culprits: Regulation, De-risking, and Technological Stagnation

So who's to blame for this mess? Like any good mystery, it's a combination of factors conspiring together:

- **Stricter Regulations**: In a post-9/11 world, AML and CTF regulations have tightened. While well-intentioned, these rules have made correspondent banking relationships more burdensome to maintain.
- **De-risking by Larger Banks**: Facing increased compliance costs and fearing hefty fines, big banks have decided that some relationships just aren't worth the hassle. It's like ending a friendship because your pal lives too far away and gas is too expensive.
- **Lack of Innovation**: While fintech startups are busy reinventing the wheel with apps that can do everything except make you breakfast, the correspondent banking system remains stuck in the technological equivalent of the Stone Age. Fax machines and manual processing, anyone?

The Domino Effect: Consequences Beyond the Ledger

The decline in correspondent banking relationships doesn't just inconvenience a few banks; it has ripple effects that spread far and wide:

- **Financial Exclusion**: Small banks, especially in developing countries, find themselves cut off from the global financial system. Their clients—often the most vulnerable populations—are left without access to essential services.
- **Stifled Economic Growth**: When businesses can't transact efficiently across borders, trade slows down. Less trade means fewer jobs, reduced GDP growth, and a perpetuation of poverty cycles.

- **Increased Illicit Activity**: Ironically, by cutting off legitimate banking channels, de-risking can push transactions into the shadows, making it harder to monitor and combat illegal activities.

Seeking Solutions: Time to Upgrade the System

But all is not lost. The correspondent banking conundrum, while complex, isn't insurmountable. Here's a thought: what if we dragged the system kicking and screaming into the 21st century?

- **Embracing Technology**: **Blockchain**, anyone? Distributed ledger technology can offer faster, cheaper, and more transparent cross-border transactions. It's not just for cryptocurrency cowboys and NFT enthusiasts; it has real-world applications that could revolutionize correspondent banking.
- **Digital Identity Verification**: Implementing robust digital identities can streamline KYC processes, reducing compliance costs and making it easier for banks to maintain relationships without sacrificing security.
- **Regulatory Collaboration**: Regulators and banks need to get on the same page. By working together to create sensible frameworks that balance risk management with practical operations, they can prevent overzealous de-risking.
- **Inclusivity Over Exclusivity**: Instead of cutting off higher-risk jurisdictions, banks could adopt a more nuanced approach. Enhanced due diligence doesn't have to mean exclusion; it can be a pathway to inclusion with safeguards.

Fostering Collaboration: All Hands on Deck

Innovation doesn't occur in a vacuum. Banks, fintech companies, regulators, and even customers must collaborate to reshape correspondent banking. **Public-private partnerships** can drive the development of common standards and protocols, ensuring interoperability and fostering trust.

Regulators play a pivotal role by providing clear guidelines that encourage innovation while safeguarding stability. By engaging with industry players, they can craft policies that reflect the realities of modern finance rather than clinging to outdated models.

Promoting Inclusivity: Leaving No One Adrift

A reimagined correspondent banking system must prioritize inclusivity. Smaller banks and institutions in developing countries have as much right to participate in the global financial system as their larger counterparts. By lowering barriers to entry and reducing reliance on a few dominant players, the system becomes more resilient and equitable.

Financial inclusion isn't just a noble goal; it's good business. Tapping into underserved markets unlocks new opportunities and fuels economic growth. It's the difference between sailing a well-worn route and discovering new worlds rich with potential.

Reimagining Correspondent Relationships: A New Map

The traditional hub-and-spoke model of correspondent banking can be replaced with a **decentralized network**, leveraging technology to connect institutions directly. This peer-to-peer approach reduces costs and delays, minimizes points of failure, and democratizes access.

It's akin to moving from a rigid fleet formation to a flotilla of agile vessels, each capable of charting its own course yet connected through shared communication and objectives.

The Role of Compliance: Navigating Safely

As we embrace innovation, compliance remains the compass guiding us away from treacherous waters. Technology enhances our ability to adhere to regulations, but it doesn't replace the need for sound judgment and ethical conduct.

By integrating compliance into the fabric of new systems—**compliance by design**—we ensure that safeguards are not afterthoughts but foundational elements. This proactive approach builds trust with regulators and customers, smoothing the path for adoption and growth.

Setting Sail for a New Horizon

Correspondent banking doesn't have to be the aging ship struggling to stay afloat. With vision, collaboration, and a willingness to embrace change, it can become a sleek, modern vessel charting a course toward a more connected and inclusive financial world.

The horizon is vast and filled with possibilities. By keeping our eyes fixed on the stars of innovation and our hands steady on the wheel of compliance, we can navigate the complexities ahead.

After all, the true essence of banking is about connections—between people, businesses, and nations. It's time we build a system that reflects that ideal, unencumbered by outdated limitations and ready to meet the demands of a new era.

Dancing to a New Tune

Correspondent banking is a complex dance requiring grace, precision, and a keen awareness of the ever-changing rhythm of global finance. Compliance isn't just a set of rules to follow; it's the choreography that ensures everyone moves in harmony.

As we navigate this intricate performance, we must remain vigilant, innovative, and ethically grounded. Because in this dance, a misstep doesn't just embarrass you—it can bring the whole ensemble crashing down.

So here's to keeping the music playing, the dancers in sync, and the audience—businesses and individuals worldwide—enjoying the show, even if they never see the intricate ballet happening behind the scenes.

Chapter 7: Digital Identity—Who Are You When Nobody Knows Your Name?

In an era where you can order a pizza, attend a meeting, and adopt a virtual pet—all without leaving your couch—it's safe to say we're living in the digital age. But with great connectivity comes great confusion, especially when it comes to **digital identity**. After all, on the internet, nobody knows you're a dog—or a cybercriminal, for that matter.

The Evolution from Usernames to Unique IDs

Remember when your online identity was just a clever username and a pixelated avatar? Simpler times. Today, digital identity has morphed into a complex tapestry woven from biometrics, cryptographic keys, and data points that would make a statistician swoon.

Advancements in technology have given us the tools to create digital representations of ourselves that are as unique as our fingerprints—quite literally. **Biometrics** like facial recognition and fingerprint scans ensure that you are who you say you are, unless, of course, you're an identical twin with a mischievous streak.

Blockchain and **decentralized identifiers (DIDs)** add layers of security and privacy, promising a world where you control your own data. It's like having a vault that only you can open, unless someone figures out a way to hack it—but let's not dwell on that.

Compliance Gets a Makeover

For compliance officers who've spent years buried under piles of paperwork verifying identities, digital identity is the breath of fresh air they've been gasping for. **KYC/AML** processes become faster, more accurate, and—dare we say it—almost enjoyable.

No more squinting at blurry photocopies of passports or deciphering questionable handwriting. Digital identity allows for instant verification, reducing fraud and freeing up time to focus on more pressing matters, like what flavor of coffee to stock in the break room.

Empowering the Individual (But Don't Get Carried Away)

One of the most revolutionary aspects of digital identity is the shift in control. Individuals can now decide what information to share and with whom. It's like being the bouncer of your own personal nightclub—you control the guest list.

This empowerment is a double-edged sword. While it's great to have control over your data, it also means you bear the responsibility of safeguarding it. Lose your digital keys, and you might find yourself locked out of your own life.

Applications: The Sky's the Limit

Digital identity isn't just for logging into your favorite streaming service. It has far-reaching applications:

- **Financial Services**: Secure access to banking, investments, and insurance without the usual rigmarole.
- **Government Services**: Imagine renewing your driver's license without spending half a day at the DMV. A utopian dream?
- **International Transactions**: Seamless cross-border interactions without the bureaucratic nightmare. Yes, please.
- **Online Voting**: A secure way to participate in democracy from your couch, assuming we can solve the challenges of verifying that the dog isn't voting.

The Hurdles: It's Not All Sunshine and Rainbows

Despite the promise, digital identity faces significant challenges:

- **Interoperability**: With so many systems and standards, getting them to play nice is like herding cats—digital cats, no less.
- **Privacy Concerns**: Handing over your biometric data requires a level of trust that not everyone is willing to extend, especially after watching one too many dystopian sci-fi films.
- **Regulatory Uncertainty**: Laws haven't quite caught up with technology, leading to a Wild West atmosphere where everyone waits for the sheriff to arrive.

The Future: A Digital Identity Renaissance

Looking ahead, digital identity is poised to revolutionize how we interact with the world—and each other. Technologies like **zero-knowledge proofs (ZKPs)** promise to enhance privacy by allowing verification without revealing actual data. It's like proving you can sing without anyone hearing your voice—a neat trick if you can pull it off.

Decentralized autonomous organizations (DAOs) may leverage digital identity to create new governance models, potentially reshaping everything from corporations to communities.

Embracing the Inevitable

Digital identity isn't just a trend; it's an evolution in how we define ourselves in a connected world. For compliance professionals, it's both a blessing and a challenge—a tool that can streamline processes while introducing new complexities.

As we hurtle toward this digital frontier, one thing is clear: identity is no longer just about who you are, but also about how you manage the myriad facets of your digital self.

So, the next time you're prompted to verify your identity with a fingerprint, a facial scan, or perhaps a DNA sample (coming soon

to a device near you), take a moment to appreciate the marvel—
and the madness—of digital identity.

Because in the end, we're all just bits and bytes in the grand
server of life, trying to ensure that we are, indeed, who we say we
are.

Chapter 8: High-Risk Banking vs. Shadow Banking—The Financial Doppelgängers

In the convoluted world of finance, terms often get tossed around
like confetti at a parade—bright, colorful, and landing who-knows-
where. Two such terms are **high-risk banking** and **shadow
banking**. They might sound like twins separated at birth, but dig a
little deeper, and you'll find they're more like distant cousins—one
trying to make an honest living, the other operating with a wink and
a nod.

High-Risk Banking: The Tightrope Walkers

High-risk banks are the adrenaline junkies of the financial sector.
They serve clients that make traditional banks sweat—
cryptocurrency exchanges, cannabis businesses, startups in
volatile regions. These banks operate fully within the regulated
system, but they like to live on the edge, taking calculated risks
that others shy away from.

They adhere to strict compliance regulations, often going above
and beyond to prove they're not the bad apples. Think of them as
the stunt performers of banking—taking risks, but with safety nets
firmly in place. They perform their high-wire acts under the big top,
with the audience (and regulators) watching every move.

Shadow Banking: The Enigmatic Strangers at the Party

Shadow banks, on the other hand, are the mysterious guests who slipped into the party without an invitation. They provide banking-like services but operate outside the traditional regulatory framework. Hedge funds, special investment vehicles, and certain fintech companies often fall into this category.

These entities thrive in the gray areas, unburdened by the regulations that keep traditional banks awake at night. Transparency isn't their forte; opacity is part of the allure. They're the speakeasies of finance—if you know, you know, but don't expect a sign on the door.

Spot the Difference: It's All in the Open (or Not)

- **Regulatory Oversight**: High-risk banks are under the regulatory microscope, while shadow banks operate in peripheral vision.
- **Transparency**: High-risk banks disclose their operations, client lists, and risk assessments. Shadow banks? They prefer to keep the curtains drawn.
- **Systemic Risk**: Shadow banks can pose significant risks to the financial system due to their size and lack of oversight. High-risk banks aim to mitigate risk through compliance, even while dealing with riskier clients.

Why It Matters: The Thin Line Between Risk and Recklessness

Understanding the distinction isn't just academic; it's crucial for regulators, investors, and anyone who doesn't want the financial system to implode—again.

High-risk banks play a vital role by providing services to sectors that might otherwise be pushed into the shadows. By operating transparently and adhering to regulations, they help prevent the very opacity that makes shadow banking so perilous.

Shadow banks, meanwhile, can contribute to systemic risk. Remember the 2008 financial crisis? Shadow banking played a starring role in that drama.

Compliance Implications: Navigating the Labyrinth

For high-risk banks, compliance is both a challenge and a shield. They must navigate complex regulations, conduct enhanced due diligence, and often deal with skepticism from regulators and the public. But their commitment to transparency and regulation can set them apart in a positive way.

Shadow banks face fewer compliance burdens, which might seem like a competitive advantage—until the lack of oversight leads to problems. When things go south, shadow banks can become the Achilles' heel of the financial system.

Choose Your Dance Partner Wisely

In the grand ballroom of finance, high-risk banks are the daring yet disciplined dancers, pushing boundaries but respecting the rules of the floor. Shadow banks are the enigmatic figures lurking in the corners, tempting but potentially treacherous.

For those in the industry, understanding the difference is key to making informed decisions. For regulators, it's about striking the right balance between encouraging innovation and preventing instability.

So the next time someone conflates high-risk banking with shadow banking, feel free to set the record straight. After all, in a world awash with financial jargon and complexity, clarity is a commodity worth its weight in gold—or perhaps in Bitcoin.

Chapter 9: The Rise of the High-Risk Client— Banking's New Normal

In the ever-evolving circus of global finance, the term **"high-risk client"** has become the elephant in the room—impossible to ignore and potentially hazardous if mishandled. But unlike the circus, there's no ringmaster here, just a lot of clowns juggling regulatory chainsaws.

Who Invited Them? Expanding the Guest List

Once upon a time, high-risk clients were easily identifiable—think arms dealers, offshore gambling operators, or anyone whose business model involved a nondescript warehouse and a lack of daylight.

But the definition has ballooned like a tech bubble. Today, high-risk clients include:

- **Cryptocurrency Entrepreneurs**: Visionaries or villains, depending on whom you ask.
- **Cannabis Industry Players**: Legal in some places, taboo in others—a compliance headache everywhere.
- **Politically Exposed Persons (PEPs)**: Because who doesn't love navigating the labyrinth of international politics?
- **Businesses in Unstable Regions**: Operating where laws are suggestions and stability is a pipe dream.

High-risk clients face a banking world that's about as welcoming as a porcupine in a balloon factory. Opening accounts becomes an epic quest, international transactions resemble a game of "Mother, May I?", and loans are guarded like the Holy Grail.

Banks, wary of regulatory backlash and reputational damage, often employ the "better safe than sorry" approach—also known as "thanks, but no thanks."

George Robson from (ex- Revolut.VC mafia) Sequoia Capital shared an exciting piece why they're backing nsave (it's awesome to see VCs getting more into the "abnormal banking" or high-risk compliance scene).

Remember the days when most investors (looking at you, USA and UK) scratched their heads over why anyone would need something like ArivalBank.com? Well, those days are behind us.

nsave is here to shake things up by offering secure and accessible offshore accounts to folks who really need them. While many in the U.S. and Europe enjoy financial stability, there are countless others in struggling economies (as 550 mln people from 15 sanctioned countries) who can barely hold onto their savings thanks to shaky banking systems, withdrawal limits, and crazy inflation. Before nsave, safe havens like USD, Euros, or GBP accounts were a dream for the wealthy. But now, thanks to nsave's smart use of Switzerland's fintech-friendly laws, everyone's got a shot at keeping their money safe.

With Sequoia Capital's backing and a spot in the Sequoia's Arc program, nsave's on a path to do more than just basic banking services; they're looking to build up financial resilience and equality on a global scale. George is all praises for the team's ability to wade through tough regulations and team up with banks, hopeful that nsave will make a huge difference in making finance more accessible to millions worldwide. By teaming up with regulated financial partners and rolling out a user-friendly app, nsave is tackling traditional risk assessments head-on, offering a lifeline to those in financial turmoil, especially in places like Lebanon, where the financial situation is dire. Here's to hoping nsave's journey brings a glimmer of hope to millions looking to keep their wealth safe and sound!

Opportunities: The Untapped Goldmine

But where some see peril, others see potential. Serving high-risk clients isn't just about dodging pitfalls; it's about tapping into a market that's underserved and overflowing with opportunity.

Financial institutions willing to navigate this minefield can:

- **Expand Their Client Base**: Be the oasis in the desert of banking options.
- **Offer Specialized Services**: Tailored compliance solutions, cross-border facilitation, and more.

- **Build a Reputation for Innovation**: Stand out in a crowded market by embracing complexity.

Compliance: The Compass and the Map

Successfully serving high-risk clients requires a compliance framework that's both robust and agile—a combination as rare as a unicorn with a day job.

Key strategies include:

- **Enhanced Due Diligence**: Go beyond checking boxes; understand the client's business inside and out.
- **Dynamic Monitoring**: Real-time tracking of transactions to spot anomalies faster than a Twitter scandal spreads.
- **Regulatory Engagement**: Proactively work with regulators to ensure transparency and build trust.

The Future: Adapt or Fade Away

The rise of high-risk clients isn't a passing fad; it's the new reality. Industries once considered fringe are moving toward the mainstream, and the financial sector must adapt or risk obsolescence.

Embracing high-risk clients isn't about throwing caution to the wind; it's about recognizing the shifting landscape and adjusting sails accordingly.

Embracing the Challenge

The financial world is at a crossroads. The traditional risk-averse path is safe but leads to stagnation. Venturing into high-risk territory offers growth but demands diligence and innovation.

For those willing to rise to the occasion, the rewards are significant—a diversified client base, enhanced expertise, and a competitive edge.

In the end, high-risk clients aren't just a challenge; they're an invitation to evolve. And in a world where change is the only constant, evolution isn't just desirable—it's essential.

Chapter 10: Compliance and Innovation at the Crossroads—Finding Harmony in Chaos

In the grand symphony of finance, **compliance** and **innovation** have often played discordant tunes. Compliance is the stern conductor insisting on adherence to the score, while innovation is the jazz soloist riffing unpredictably. But as the financial landscape evolves, it's clear that these two must find a harmonious duet to navigate the complexities of the modern world.

From Necessary Evil to Strategic Asset

Once relegated to the back office with the excitement level of watching paint dry, compliance has undergone a metamorphosis. It's no longer just about avoiding fines or appeasing regulators with a well-organized binder of policies. Today, compliance is a strategic asset, a competitive differentiator that can propel businesses forward.

Institutions like **ArivalBank.com** have demonstrated that proactive compliance isn't a hindrance but a catalyst for growth. By integrating compliance into the core strategy, they've transformed it from a box-ticking exercise into a value-adding function.

Proactive Compliance: The New Norm

Reactive compliance—scrambling to fix issues after they've been flagged—is about as effective as locking the barn door after the horse has bolted. The modern approach is proactive, anticipating risks and addressing them before they become problems.

Investing in advanced technologies like **blockchain**, **artificial intelligence**, and **machine learning** allows institutions to monitor transactions in real-time, detect anomalies, and make informed decisions swiftly. This isn't just about staying out of trouble; it's about building trust and credibility in an industry where reputation is everything.

Innovation's Role in Compliance

Innovation isn't the rebellious teenager testing curfews anymore; it's the ally helping compliance teams work smarter, not harder. Technologies that were once viewed with suspicion are now indispensable tools in the compliance arsenal.

- **Artificial Intelligence**: AI algorithms can analyze vast datasets faster than you can say "regulatory breach," identifying patterns that humans might miss.
- **Digital Identity Solutions**: Tools like **Nansen.ID** streamline KYC processes, reducing friction for clients while enhancing verification accuracy.
- **Blockchain Technology**: With its transparent and immutable ledger, blockchain offers a robust platform for recording transactions, making audits less of a nightmare and more of a formality.

By embracing these innovations, financial institutions can enhance their compliance efforts, reduce costs, and improve customer experiences—a trifecta of benefits that's hard to ignore.

Global Implications: A Unified Front Against Financial Crime

Compliance-driven innovation isn't just beneficial for individual institutions; it has global ramifications. By raising the bar for compliance standards worldwide, we create a less hospitable environment for fraud, money laundering, and other illicit activities.

Moreover, technological advancements can extend financial services to underserved populations, promoting inclusion and economic development. It's a win-win scenario where doing good aligns with doing well.

Challenges on the Horizon

Of course, marrying compliance and innovation isn't without its challenges. Ethical considerations, data privacy concerns, and the potential for technological misuse require vigilant oversight.

- **Data Privacy**: Balancing the need for information with the right to privacy is a tightrope walk that requires careful policy crafting and transparent practices.
- **Cybersecurity**: As systems become more interconnected, they also become more vulnerable to attacks. Robust security measures are non-negotiable.
- **Regulatory Adaptation**: Laws and regulations must evolve alongside technology, a process that can feel like steering a cargo ship with a canoe paddle.

Crafting a Collaborative Future

At the crossroads of compliance and innovation lies an opportunity—a chance to redefine how the financial industry operates. By viewing compliance not as a hurdle but as a partner, institutions can foster environments where innovation thrives within ethical boundaries.

The key is collaboration. Regulators, financial institutions, technologists, and even customers must engage in open dialogue to navigate the complexities ahead. Together, they can develop frameworks that encourage innovation while safeguarding against risks.

In the end, the goal isn't just to avoid the next **Wirecard** scandal but to build a financial ecosystem that is resilient, inclusive, and trustworthy. It's a lofty ambition, but one worth striving for. Because when compliance and innovation dance in step, the music they create isn't just harmonious—it's transformative.

Chapter 11: The Compliance Unlikely Hero

Creating a bank from scratch is a bit like assembling a spaceship in your garage—you need innovation, precision, and a touch of audacity. **ArivalBank.com** wasn't just any bank; it was our meticulously designed fortress of compliance, a beacon for high-risk clients shunned by the buttoned-up traditional banks. We didn't just color within the lines; we redrew them to create a masterpiece of modern banking. And for a while, it stood tall and proud.

A Sanctuary for the Financially Misunderstood

Imagine a place where cryptocurrency entrepreneurs, fintech innovators, and other financial mavericks could find a banking home. That's what we envisioned with ArivalBank.com—a sanctuary for those exiled by conventional institutions more comfortable with cookie-cutter clients.

Our mission was audacious: to prove that high-risk banking didn't have to be synonymous with high drama. We embedded compliance into every fiber of our operations. It wasn't a department; it was our DNA. We didn't see compliance as a chore but as an art form—a competitive advantage that set us apart.

Clients loved it. They weren't just account numbers; they were partners in a grand experiment to redefine banking. We offered them transparency, security, and a level of service that made them wonder why they ever tolerated the old guard's disdain.

Turning Red Tape into a Red Carpet

While other banks saw compliance as a ball and chain, we turned it into a red carpet, welcoming clients with open arms and robust safeguards. **Compliance-as-a-Service (CaaS)** wasn't just a buzzword; it was our secret sauce.

We harnessed cutting-edge technologies—AI-driven risk assessments, real-time transaction monitoring, and open-source intelligence tools that Sherlock Holmes would envy. Our approach transformed compliance from a necessary evil into a selling point. Clients didn't just tolerate our thorough vetting; they celebrated it. After all, in a world rife with financial skullduggery, who wouldn't want a bank that treated security like the crown jewels?

Navigating the Regulatory Jungle

Securing a banking license is challenging at the best of times; doing so while intending to serve high-risk clients is like trying to get a license to drive a rocket ship—on Mars. We faced skepticism from regulators who had visions of money laundering and compliance nightmares dancing in their heads.

Undeterred, we embarked on a mission to demonstrate that high-risk didn't have to mean non-compliant. We invested heavily in building a compliance infrastructure that could withstand the scrutiny of even the most exacting regulators.

Establishing correspondent banking relationships was another Everest to climb. Traditional banks, wary of reputational risk, were hesitant to partner with an institution catering to the financial world's mavericks. It was a bit like asking a prim and proper debutante to attend a rock concert. Yet, through persistence and demonstrating our unwavering commitment to compliance, we secured the necessary partnerships.

Compliance by Design: The Heart of Innovation

At ArivalBank.com, compliance wasn't the department that threw cold water on innovation; it was the engine that powered it. We adopted a **"compliance by design"** approach, integrating regulatory requirements into the very fabric of our systems and services.

Utilizing advanced technologies like artificial intelligence, machine learning, and blockchain, we developed sophisticated **Know Your**

Customer (KYC) and **Anti-Money Laundering (AML)** protocols. These weren't just fancy buzzwords to impress investors; they were practical tools that allowed us to monitor transactions in real-time, detect anomalies, and manage risks proactively.

This approach turned compliance from a burdensome obligation into a competitive advantage. Clients appreciated the transparency and the assurance that they were dealing with a bank that took integrity seriously. In a world where trust is often in short supply, our commitment to compliance became one of our most valuable assets.

Serving the Underserved: More Than a Mission Statement

We didn't just open our doors to high-risk clients; we rolled out the red carpet. We provided tailored solutions for cryptocurrency exchanges, fintech startups, and international businesses that struggled to find banking services elsewhere.

Our digital platform was designed with the user in mind—intuitive, accessible, and efficient. Account opening processes that took weeks at traditional banks were streamlined to days, without sacrificing due diligence. Cross-border transactions, often a labyrinthine ordeal, were simplified through partnerships and innovative technology integrations.

By addressing the unique needs of our clients, we weren't just filling a market gap; we were fostering an ecosystem where innovation could thrive. We proved that serving high-risk clients didn't have to equate to higher risk for the bank itself.

Lessons Learned: The Highs, Lows, and In-Betweens

Our journey was anything but smooth sailing. We faced challenges that would have made lesser institutions throw in the towel. Regulatory landscapes shifted like desert sands, technology evolved at breakneck speeds, and global events introduced unforeseen hurdles.

One of the key lessons was the importance of agility. We had to remain nimble, adapting quickly to new regulations, market demands, and technological advancements. This flexibility became a core strength, allowing us to stay ahead of competitors and maintain compliance in a dynamic environment.

Another lesson was the critical role of education—not just internally but also for our clients. Many high-risk clients were pioneers in their fields but lacked understanding of the complex regulatory requirements. We took on the role of educator, helping clients navigate the compliance maze, which in turn strengthened our relationships and mutual trust.

Charting a New Course in Banking

ArivalBank.com stood as a testament to what is possible when bold vision meets unwavering commitment to compliance and innovation. We challenged the status quo, proving that a bank could serve high-risk clients responsibly and profitably.

Our story is more than a case study in fintech; it's a narrative about the future of banking—a future where inclusivity, technology, and integrity coexist harmoniously. We didn't just build a bank; we built a blueprint for how financial institutions can adapt and thrive in a rapidly changing world.

Part II. **From Wirecard to Tether: Inside the World's Financial Scandals and the Battle for Transparency**

Chapter 12: The Fintech Icarus of Wirecard— The Unicorn That Sprouted Wings and Flew Too Close to the Sun

Once upon a time in the glittering world of fintech, there was a company named **Wirecard**. It wasn't just any company; it was Germany's pride and joy, the prodigious offspring that was supposed to put European fintech on the global map. Backed by heavyweight investors, endorsed by politicians, and adored by the media, Wirecard was the wunderkind that could do no wrong.

But as any good Greek tragedy will tell you, hubris is a dangerous thing.

The Meteoric Rise: When the Sky Wasn't the Limit

Wirecard started in the early 2000s, positioning itself as the edgy disruptor among stodgy old banks. It promised innovation, agility, and a sprinkle of techno-magic that would revolutionize payments. With partnerships spanning from global giants to corner-store merchants, Wirecard seemed unstoppable.

They weren't just thinking outside the box; they were shredding the box, setting it on fire, and dancing around the flames. Investors threw money at them faster than you could say "due diligence," and regulators gave them the kind of free pass usually reserved for celebrities at exclusive nightclubs.

Enter Jan Marsalek: The Man, The Myth, The Mystery

At the heart of this whirlwind was **Jan Marsalek**, the enigmatic COO and the <u>Money Men</u>[10] whose charisma could charm the spots off a leopard. Marsalek was the James Bond of fintech, minus the license to kill but possibly with a license to thrill auditors into looking the other way.

Rumors swirled about his connections—from international espionage to clandestine meetings that would make a spy novelist blush. He was the kind of figure who made you wonder if he attended board meetings via secret tunnels while stroking a white cat.

The Cracks in the Facade: Journalists Crash the Party

While everyone was busy applauding Wirecard's skyrocketing success, a few pesky journalists at the *Financial Times* started asking inconvenient questions. You know, minor things like "Where is the profit actually coming from?" and "Why do some of these subsidiaries seem to exist only on paper?"

Wirecard responded with the grace of a cornered raccoon. Legal threats flew, defamation lawsuits piled up, and critics were branded as conspirators aiming to undermine Germany's fintech gem. It was a classic case of "methinks thou doth protest too much."

The Great Unraveling: When Billions Vanish

In June 2020, the fairy tale took a dark turn. Wirecard admitted that **€1.9 billion** was missing. Not "misplaced" or "tied up in assets"—just gone, like a magician's rabbit. Except this trick didn't leave the audience applauding.

---

[10] https://amzn.to/3YxUfNt

The money was supposedly held in accounts in the Philippines, but authorities there looked around and said, "Nope, haven't seen it." Cue the collective facepalm of investors, regulators, and anyone who had ever sung Wirecard's praises.

Markus Braun resigned in disgrace, his minimalist wardrobe suddenly less chic. Meanwhile, Jan Marsalek [Jan Marsalek: from Wirecard to Putin's spy[11]] vanished entirely, leaving behind more questions than answers. His disappearance added a layer of international intrigue that even spy novelists might find over-the-top.

The Fallout: A Wake-Up Call for the Financial World

Wirecard's collapse was seismic. Investors were left clutching worthless shares, regulators faced harsh scrutiny, and Germany's reputation for meticulous efficiency took a hit. The scandal highlighted glaring weaknesses in oversight and due diligence, not just in Germany but across global financial markets.

It was a stark reminder that innovation without integrity is a perilous path. Wirecard had mastered the art of appearing revolutionary while allegedly engaging in age-old deceit. The fintech emperor, it turned out, had no clothes.

Lessons Etched in Infamy

Wirecard's debacle serves as a cautionary tale for our times. It underscores the necessity of rigorous compliance, transparent governance, and the courage to question even the most dazzling success stories. In a world enamored with innovation, we must remember that progress built on deception is destined to crumble.

For investors, regulators, and innovators alike, Wirecard's story is a sobering reminder: when something seems too good to be true,

---

[11] https://www.slideshare.net/slideshow/jan-marsalek-from-wirecard-to-putin-s-spy/272942314

it just might be. And in the high-stakes game of global finance, due diligence isn't just a formality—it's a lifeline.

Rebuilding on Solid Ground

The fall of Wirecard shook the foundations of fintech but also paved the way for reform. By learning from these failures, the industry can implement safeguards that prevent similar deceptions.

Transparency, accountability, and a commitment to ethical standards are not obstacles to success but the pillars upon which sustainable innovation is built. As fintech continues to evolve, these principles will be essential in guiding the next generation of companies toward a future where technology and trust go hand in hand.

The Fine Line Between Visionary and Illusionist

Wirecard wanted to be a pioneer, but they chose the path of illusion over integrity. They didn't just blur the lines between high-risk and shadow banking; they danced across them with reckless abandon.

Their story reinforces the importance of transparency, accountability, and, yes, good old-fashioned compliance. Because at the end of the day, no amount of charm or ambition can replace the foundational trust that holds the financial system together.

The Aftermath: Picking Up the Pieces

In the wake of the scandal, Germany's financial watchdogs faced intense scrutiny. How could this happen under their noses? The incident spurred calls for stricter regulations, better oversight, and perhaps a refresher course in not taking companies at their word when billions are unaccounted for.

For the rest of us in the fintech world, Wirecard's downfall served as a stark reminder: innovation without integrity is a recipe for disaster. It's like building a skyscraper without a solid foundation—

it might reach impressive heights, but it's only a matter of time before gravity has its say.

When Innovation Takes a Detour

Wirecard's implosion wasn't just a corporate failure; it was a systemic one. It highlighted how charisma and rapid growth could blind regulators, investors, and the public to glaring red flags. At ArivalBank.com, we watched this saga unfold with a mix of horror and validation. Horror at the scale of the deception, and validation of our steadfast commitment to compliance. Wirecard was the antithesis of everything we stand for—a cautionary tale of what happens when compliance is treated as an obstacle rather than a foundation.

Their story serves as a stark reminder that innovation must be grounded in integrity. Charismatic leaders and impressive growth trajectories cannot substitute for sound business practices and ethical conduct. Because at the end of the day, trust isn't just a buzzword—it's the currency that keeps the entire financial system afloat.

Chapter 13: ENRC—Mining for Riches or Digging a Hole?

In the high-stakes world of global finance, some companies play by the rules, others bend them, and then there's the **Eurasian Natural Resources Corporation (ENRC)**—which seemed to have tossed the rulebook into one of their mines and buried it deeper than their deepest shaft.

A Glittering Empire Built on Shaky Ground

ENRC [From ENRC to Arival: The Oligarch's Shadow Over Singapore Courts[12]] wasn't your run-of-the-mill mining outfit. With vast holdings stretching across Africa and Central Asia, they weren't just unearthing minerals—they were excavating profits in regions where laws were more like polite suggestions than actual constraints.

Operating in countries with more coups than successful elections, ENRC mastered the art of navigating "flexible" regulatory environments. They maneuvered through the shadows, leveraging offshore accounts and complex ownership structures that could make even the most seasoned tax attorney weep with envy—or perhaps frustration.

Their philosophy was refreshingly straightforward: if transparency was optional, they'd happily opt out. After all, why let a little thing like accountability get in the way of a good profit margin?

Shadow Banking: The Preferred Currency of the Unaccountable

To fuel their ambitious ventures, ENRC tapped into the world of **shadow banking**—that elusive network of unregulated financial activities operating just beyond the reach of traditional oversight. Think of it as the dark web of finance, but with fewer hackers and more bespoke suits.

Shadow banking allowed ENRC to move money across borders with the grace of a ballerina and the stealth of a ninja. Need to pay a "facilitation fee" to a local official? Consider it done. Want to acquire a rival company without those pesky antitrust authorities noticing? Easy as pie.

But as any good spy movie will tell you, operating in the shadows comes with risks. ENRC was about to discover that shadows can conceal dangers just as well as they hide secrets.

Journalists: Flashlights in the Darkness

---

[12] https://www.linkedin.com/pulse/from-enrc-arival-oligarchs-shadow-over-singapore-courts-solodkiy-y0qfe/

Enter the intrepid journalists from *The Financial Times* and *The Guardian*—the uninvited guests who show up just when the party is getting interesting. They began digging into ENRC's operations, unearthing allegations of bribery, corruption, and environmental devastation that would make even a supervillain blush.

ENRC responded with all the subtlety of a bull in a china shop. They unleashed a barrage of legal threats, defamation suits, and enough intimidation tactics to fill a thriller novel. Their mission was clear: silence the critics and keep those skeletons firmly locked in the closet.

But journalists are a tenacious breed. The more ENRC pushed back, the deeper they dug. It became a classic game of cat and mouse—except this time, the mouse had a global media platform, and the cat was increasingly cornered.

Compliance? Never Heard of It

ENRC's disregard for compliance wasn't just a business strategy—it was practically a corporate mantra. Why bother with pesky regulations when you can operate with impunity in jurisdictions where the rule of law is more of a guideline?

Their tactics highlighted a glaring issue in global finance: the ease with which companies can exploit regulatory loopholes, especially in high-risk [High-Risk Compliance for BaaS and Correspondent Banks[13]] regions. It's like playing Monopoly with invisible dice and a Get Out of Jail Free card that works every time.

The Fallout: When the House of Cards Collapses

Eventually, the pressure became too great. Investigations by the UK's **Serious Fraud Office (SFO)** and other agencies began peeling back the layers of ENRC's operations. Allegations ranged

---

[13] https://www.linkedin.com/pulse/high-risk-compliance-baas-correspondent-banks-vladislav-solodkiy-4eotc/

from bribery to fraud to environmental crimes that would give Captain Planet sleepless nights.

The company's reputation took a nosedive faster than a lead balloon, and investors started fleeing like rats from a sinking ship. It turns out that while profits are enticing, they're less appealing when paired with potential legal troubles and ethical quandaries.

The High Cost of Low Ethics

ENRC's saga serves as a stark reminder of the perils of unchecked ambition and the illusion of invincibility that comes from operating in the shadows. For those of us in the compliance world, it's both a cautionary tale and a vindication of why our work matters.

At **ArivalBank.com**, we took note. ENRC exemplified everything we aim to avoid—a lack of transparency, disregard for regulations, and a willingness to sacrifice ethics for profit. We reaffirmed our commitment to operating above board, even when the allure of easy gains tempts others down darker paths.

Shining a Light into the Shadows

The story of ENRC isn't just about one company's missteps; it's a reflection of systemic issues in global finance. As long as shadow banking and unregulated practices exist, so too will the temptations and pitfalls that ensnared ENRC.

But there's hope. With increased transparency, robust compliance frameworks, and a commitment to ethical practices, we can begin to close the gaps that allow such behavior to flourish.

Because at the end of the day, it's better to build a smaller empire on solid ground than a vast one destined to crumble under the weight of its own deception.

Chapter 14: Tether, Deltec, and the Quest for the Crypto Shangri-La

In the swashbuckling world of high finance, few things have shaken the establishment quite like cryptocurrency. It's as if the financial wizards of the world decided to throw a rave, and everyone showed up with their own version of fun—some with glow sticks, others with questionable substances, and a few with intentions as murky as a politician's promise.

At the epicenter of this digital gold rush stands **Tether**, the so-called stablecoin pegged to the U.S. dollar. It's the reliable friend who's supposed to keep the party from spiraling out of control. But as with any good party, things aren't always what they seem once the strobe lights kick in.

Tether: The Digital Chameleon

Tether was designed to be the calm in the crypto storm—a digital asset that wouldn't swing wildly every time Elon Musk sneezed. For traders, it was a godsend. Need to park your gains without converting back to fiat currency? Tether had you covered.

But behind the veneer of stability lurked questions that would make even the most hardened accountant break into a sweat. Where were the reserves backing Tether? Were they real dollars or just IOUs scribbled on cocktail napkins?

As sanctions tightened around countries like Russia, Tether became more than just a convenience—it became a lifeline. Suddenly, it wasn't just crypto enthusiasts using Tether; it was anyone looking to move money without the pesky oversight of regulators. The stablecoin had morphed into the digital equivalent of an unmarked briefcase full of cash.

Deltec: Banking in Paradise (But Watch Your Step)

Enter **Deltec Bank**, nestled in the Bahamas—a location known for its pristine beaches, offshore accounts, and regulations as laid-back as a hammock on a summer's day. Deltec [Follow The Money: Brock Pierce, Tether, Deltec, FTX[14]] became the proud custodian of Tether's reserves, or at least that's what we were told.

For a small bank in a tropical paradise to hold billions in reserves raised eyebrows higher than a botched Botox job. Skeptics wondered how this boutique institution ended up at the center of the crypto universe. Optimists believed it was a sign of the democratization of finance. Realists grabbed the popcorn and waited for the next act.

Deltec embraced its role with open arms and perhaps a Mai Tai in hand. It catered to crypto companies and high-risk clients who found traditional banks about as welcoming as a tax audit. In the Bahamas, where the motto might as well be "What happens here stays under wraps," Deltec provided services that others wouldn't dare touch.

Puerto Rico: The Crypto Casanova

While Deltec was turning heads in the Bahamas, **Puerto Rico** [Estonian Metastate Experience for Puerto Rico and Other Territories[15]] was busy reinventing itself as the "Crypto Island." With tax incentives that made millionaires giggle like schoolchildren, it attracted a wave of crypto enthusiasts, entrepreneurs, and the occasional eccentric billionaire.

Why pay hefty U.S. taxes when you could sip piña coladas on a Caribbean island and keep Uncle Sam at bay? It was a no-brainer for those whose wealth was tied up in digital assets and whose patience for regulation was thinner than a blockchain ledger.

---

[14] https://www.slideshare.net/slideshow/followthemoney-brock-pierce-tether-deltec-ftx/272943361

[15] https://medium.com/@slavasolodkiy_67243/estonian-experience-for-puerto-rico-what-about-initial-country-offering-for-70b-8cc7e2656a6f

Names like **Brock Pierce** started popping up—former child actor turned crypto evangelist—adding a touch of Hollywood flair to the mix. Puerto Rico wasn't just a tax haven; it was a social experiment in what happens when you mix vast wealth, minimal oversight, and a penchant for disruption.

The Double-Edged Sword of Financial Freedom

The allure of Tether, Deltec, and Puerto Rico's tax incentives paints a vivid picture of the modern quest for financial freedom. It's like the Wild West but with better gadgets and less regard for tumbleweeds.

On one hand, these crypto havens represent innovation, a rebellion against outdated financial systems that move at the pace of a sloth in a marathon. On the other, they pose significant risks— lack of transparency, regulatory crackdowns, and the ever-looming possibility of it all collapsing like a poorly built sandcastle.

For regulators, it's a game of Whac-A-Mole played blindfolded. How do you oversee an industry designed to be ungovernable? For high-risk clients, it's a thrilling ride with the ever-present danger of flying off the rails.

Reality Bites: The Risks of Playing in the Shadows

As governments around the world start paying closer attention, the noose tightens. Accusations of market manipulation, concerns over Tether's reserves, and the precarious nature of banking partnerships like Deltec's make for a suspenseful drama.

Will Tether maintain its peg if confidence wavers? What happens if regulators decide they've had enough of the crypto shenanigans and bring down the hammer? These questions keep investors up at night, pondering whether their digital fortunes are built on solid ground or shifting sands.

Navigating the Crypto Frontier

The saga of Tether, Deltec, and Puerto Rico is a microcosm of the larger crypto narrative—a blend of innovation, ambition, and a dash of audacity. It's a world where fortunes can be made overnight, and lost just as quickly.

For those of us in the compliance sphere, it reinforces the importance of transparency and due diligence. The glitter of potential profits shouldn't blind us to the risks lurking in the shadows. As the saying goes, not all that glitters is gold—or in this case, not every stablecoin is as stable as it claims.

The crypto frontier is far from settled territory. It's an ever-evolving landscape that challenges our notions of finance, regulation, and even reality itself. Whether it's a revolution or a reckless gamble remains to be seen. One thing is certain: it's a story that continues to unfold, and we're all along for the ride—whether we like it or not.

Chapter 15: Tether—The Stablecoin with a Loose Grip on Stability

In the rollercoaster world of cryptocurrency, where values swing like a pendulum in a hurricane, **Tether (USDT)** emerged as the supposed voice of reason—a stablecoin promising to hold steady amidst the chaos. Pegged to the mighty U.S. dollar, Tether was the financial equivalent of a calm harbor in a stormy sea. But as with any good tale in the crypto realm, the waters run deeper than they first appear, and sometimes there's a kraken lurking beneath the surface.

The Birth of Stability in an Unstable World

Launched in 2014, Tether was one of the first stablecoins to grace the crypto stage. Its premise was simple yet revolutionary: for every Tether token issued, there would be one U.S. dollar held in reserve. It was like promising a golden ticket for every chocolate bar sold—except in this case, the chocolate bars were digital, and the golden tickets were, well, somewhat elusive.

The allure was undeniable. Traders could now move in and out of crypto positions without the need to convert back to traditional fiat currency, saving time and avoiding pesky bank fees. Tether was the bridge between the old world of tangible dollars and the new frontier of digital assets—a foot in both camps, wearing two different shoes.

The Big Fish in a Growing Pond

Tether didn't just join the party; it became the DJ. Quickly ascending to become the most traded stablecoin, USDT became the lubricant that kept the crypto markets humming. Need to buy Bitcoin? Swap for some Ethereum? Tether was there, facilitating trades with the smooth efficiency of a seasoned maître d'.

Its ubiquity made it a critical component of the crypto ecosystem. Exchanges worldwide adopted USDT as a base trading pair, and for many, it became the de facto standard for liquidity. In a market notorious for volatility, Tether was the dependable uncle who always showed up on time—until people started questioning what was in his briefcase.

The Elephant in the Blockchain

For all its popularity, Tether had a lingering question mark hovering over it like a cartoon anvil: Where exactly were all those dollars it promised to hold in reserve? Critics and skeptics—possibly the same folks who question the moon landing and insist Elvis is alive—began to poke holes in Tether's assertions.

The company's opaque disclosures didn't help. Audits were promised and then postponed or canceled. Explanations about reserve compositions shifted like sand dunes in a desert. At one point, Tether admitted that its tokens were not entirely backed by cash but by a mix of assets, including—wait for it—receivables from loans made to third parties.

It's like assuring everyone that your lemonade stand is fully stocked with lemons, only to reveal later that some of those lemons are actually IOUs from your cousin Larry.

Regulatory Scrutiny: When the Music Stops

Inevitably, the regulators came knocking. In 2021, Tether settled with the New York Attorney General's office, paying an **$18.5 million** fine for misrepresenting the degree to which its tokens were backed by fiat collateral. The investigation revealed periods when Tether had no access to banking services and made false statements about reserves.

This wasn't just a slap on the wrist; it was more like a stern lecture from a disappointed parent. Yet, the crypto markets seemed largely unfazed. Traders continued to use USDT, perhaps adopting a "don't ask, don't tell" policy or simply preferring convenience over due diligence.

The Ripple Effect on the Crypto Ecosystem

Tether's dominance means that any wobble in its stability could have seismic effects on the broader crypto market. If confidence in USDT were to falter, it could trigger a cascade of sell-offs, liquidity crunches, and a general atmosphere of panic—think of it as a digital bank run without the physical doors to lock.

Some argue that Tether is a ticking time bomb, while others believe it's too entrenched to fail. After all, if everyone agrees to keep playing the game, does it matter if the rules are a bit murky? It's a philosophical quandary worthy of a late-night dorm room discussion.

The Future of Tether: Navigating Uncharted Waters

As the regulatory environment tightens and competitors emerge with more transparent models, Tether faces an uncertain horizon. Stablecoins like **USD Coin (USDC)** offer monthly attestations and greater transparency, positioning themselves as trustworthy alternatives.

Tether has made moves to increase transparency, publishing breakdowns of its reserves and engaging with regulators. Whether these efforts are enough to restore full confidence remains to be seen. In the wild west of crypto, trust is both a precious commodity and a fragile one.

The Paradox of Trust in a Trustless System

Tether embodies the contradictions at the heart of cryptocurrency—a technology built on decentralization and transparency, yet often operating in opacity. It serves as a mirror reflecting both the ingenuity and the recklessness that can define the crypto space.

For all its flaws, Tether remains a cornerstone of the market, a testament to the community's willingness to embrace complexity and, at times, overlook inconvenient truths for the sake of convenience.

As we watch Tether navigate the challenges ahead, one can't help but be reminded of ancient mariners sailing uncharted seas. The journey is fraught with peril, the maps are incomplete, but the potential rewards keep adventurers pressing forward.

Walking Between Innovation and Integrity

In the end, Tether's story is still being written. Whether it becomes a legend of innovation or a cautionary tale of hubris will depend on its ability to adapt, embrace transparency, and earn the trust it has so long promised.

As we stand at the crossroads of financial evolution, the choices made by institutions, regulators, and users alike will shape the narrative. Will Tether emerge as a paragon of stability and openness, or will it remain a shadowy figure in the bustling marketplace of global finance?

The answer, much like the technology itself, isn't black or white but resides in the complex interplay of ethics, oversight, and the ever-shifting landscape of global finance.

Chapter 16. Deltec—Banking Under the Palm Trees

In the world of finance, location is everything. Some banks opt for the stoic grandeur of New York skyscrapers, others for the historic charm of London alleyways. And then there's **Deltec Bank & Trust**, nestled comfortably in the Bahamas—a place where the sun shines bright, the beaches are pristine, and regulatory oversight is, well, let's just say it's wearing flip-flops.

From Private Wealth to Crypto Wealth

Founded as a humble private wealth institution, Deltec spent its early years managing the fortunes of the discreetly affluent. It was the kind of place where the most significant excitement involved adjusting portfolio allocations or debating the merits of emerging markets over a round of golf.

But then the 2010s rolled in, and with them, the enigmatic allure of cryptocurrency. Under the leadership of **Jean Chalopin**, a man who apparently saw the future and decided it was digital, Deltec ventured boldly into the crypto space. After all, why stick to the predictable world of traditional banking when you can dive headfirst into an industry that combines the thrill of a rollercoaster with the opacity of a magician's trick?

Tethering to Controversy

In 2018, Deltec made headlines by becoming the banking partner for **Tether**, the stablecoin that promises each token is backed by a real U.S. dollar—somewhere, somehow. Critics have long questioned Tether's transparency, but Deltec seemed unfazed.

Perhaps they took comfort in the age-old adage: "Ignorance is bliss," or maybe they just enjoyed living dangerously.

By facilitating the issuance and redemption of **USDT**, Deltec positioned itself at the heart of the crypto liquidity engine. It's like being the bartender at a party where everyone's had a bit too much, but the drinks keep flowing, and nobody's asking for IDs.

FTX: Riding the Wave Until It Crashes

Not content with one controversial client, Deltec also became a financial hub for **FTX**, the cryptocurrency exchange that dazzled the world before collapsing in a spectacular fashion in 2022. FTX's implosion raised eyebrows, questions, and, for some, blood pressure.

Deltec's involvement with FTX has led observers to wonder about the bank's risk management practices. Did they perform due diligence, or did they just enjoy the thrill of surfing atop a tsunami? It's hard to say, but the legal challenges piling up suggest that the ride wasn't as smooth as they'd hoped.

When Risk Management Takes a Vacation

Deltec's associations have brought it under the microscope, not the best place to be when operating under the Caribbean sun. Allegations have surfaced that the bank may have been less than diligent in monitoring its clients' activities. Of course, in a place famous for its laid-back lifestyle, perhaps "due diligence" takes on a more relaxed meaning.

The bank's relationship with Tether has been particularly scrutinized. Skeptics point out that Tether's lack of transparency and alleged market manipulations are red flags the size of beach towels. Yet, Deltec seemed content to provide the umbrella drinks and let the party continue.

A Cautionary Tale for the Crypto Enthusiast

Deltec's journey serves as a modern fable for financial institutions eyeing the crypto industry with a mix of greed and trepidation. The allure of high returns and rapid growth can be tempting, but as Deltec's experience shows, the line between bold innovation and reckless abandon is thinner than a Bahamian lizard's tail. For banks considering a dip in the crypto waters, Deltec's story is a reminder to pack not just sunscreen but also a robust compliance framework. Otherwise, they might find themselves sunburned by regulatory scrutiny and legal entanglements.

Stormy Seas or Smooth Sailing?

As Deltec navigates the choppy waters of legal challenges and reputational damage, its future in the cryptocurrency space hangs in the balance. Will it chart a course towards stricter compliance and risk management, or will it double down on its high-risk, high-reward strategy? One thing is certain: the bank's ability to adapt will determine its fate. In an industry where fortunes can change with a tweet and regulations are evolving faster than fashion trends, agility and prudence are invaluable.

Paradise Lost or Found?

Deltec Bank & Trust's foray into the wild west of cryptocurrency is a story of ambition, daring, and perhaps a touch of hubris. Nestled in the idyllic Bahamas, the bank attempted to ride the crypto wave but found that the waters were teeming with unseen hazards. Their experience underscores a fundamental lesson: in finance, as in life, shortcuts can lead to dead ends. Embracing innovation is commendable, but without solid foundations in compliance and due diligence, even the most promising ventures can falter.

So, as the sun sets over Nassau, Deltec faces a crossroads. Will it emerge as a pioneer who learned from missteps, or will it become a cautionary tale whispered in the corridors of more conservative banks? Only time will tell, but one thing's for sure: the beaches may be beautiful, but in banking, paradise doesn't come without a price.

Chapter 17: Puerto Rico and the Bahamas— Islands in the Crypto Stream

Imagine paradisiacal islands with azure waters, swaying palm trees, and a tropical breeze that whispers promises of relaxation. Now, add to that image a burgeoning community of cryptocurrency enthusiasts, blockchain innovators, and fintech startups. Welcome to **Puerto Rico** and the **Bahamas**—destinations not just for tourists but also for the architects of the digital financial future.

The Lure of Paradise: Crypto Communities Take Root

Both Puerto Rico and the Bahamas offer more than scenic beauty. They present attractive tax incentives, business-friendly regulations, and a strategic location bridging North and South America. For entrepreneurs in the volatile world of cryptocurrencies, these factors create an enticing environment.

In Puerto Rico, Acts 20 and 22 offer significant tax breaks for businesses and individuals relocating to the island. The Bahamas, with its progressive regulatory framework under the Digital Assets and Registered Exchanges (DARE) Act, has positioned itself as a welcoming jurisdiction for crypto ventures.

The influx of crypto entrepreneurs has led to the emergence of vibrant communities. Co-working spaces, incubators, and networking events have sprouted, fostering collaboration and innovation. The islands have become laboratories for experimenting with blockchain applications, from finance to supply chain to real estate.

This migration brings economic opportunities, job creation, and the potential to diversify economies traditionally reliant on tourism. The infusion of tech-savvy talent can stimulate growth and position the islands as leaders in the digital economy.

Navigating Risks and Responsibilities

However, the embrace of cryptocurrency comes with challenges. The decentralized and often anonymous nature of digital assets can attract those looking to exploit vulnerabilities for money laundering, fraud, or other illicit activities.

Regulators in both Puerto Rico and the Bahamas face the task of encouraging innovation while implementing safeguards. Establishing clear guidelines, enforcing compliance with international standards, and fostering a culture of ethical conduct are essential steps.

Why does everyone primarily focus on developed markets for launching their fintechs?

There are 33 dwarf states in the world - why doesn't anyone want to start 'their Revolut or World' there?

Recently, the International Monetary Fund released a report stating that CBDCs and stablecoins could help Pacific island countries improve the accessibility and quality of financial services. They highlighted the challenges faced by "dozens" of jurisdictions and micro-states located in the Pacific Islands area: "*Limited access to financial services contributes to the persistence of poverty and inequality. These countries also depend on remittance flows, making them disproportionately affected by the reduction in interbank relationships.*" Such states could benefit from the "digital money revolution" by developing payment systems and blockchain technologies, stimulating their own economy. Interestingly, the Fund did not recommend small Pacific island countries issue their sovereign "stablecoins" due to a lack of supervisory capabilities. "*Foreign currency-based stablecoins could become a real alternative for countries without their own currency, but only under strict regulation and supervision,*" the experts emphasized. According to the document, none of the Pacific island countries use private cryptocurrency or "stablecoins" - while only Fiji, Palau, Solomon Islands, and Vanuatu are exploring CBDCs.

There are 33 small states and territories similar to the British Virgin Islands (BVI) and Panama, known for their characteristics as tax havens or offshore financial centers. Excluding Liechtenstein and Monaco, the total population of these small island and micro-states is approximately 9,155,216:

Anguilla: 15,000   Antigua and Barbuda: 97,929   Bahamas: 385,640

Building a Sustainable Ecosystem

Sustainability hinges on balance. The regulatory environment must be robust enough to deter bad actors but flexible enough to adapt to a rapidly evolving industry. Collaboration between government agencies, industry players, and international partners enhances the ability to monitor activities and respond to emerging threats.

Education and community engagement also play vital roles. By promoting awareness of best practices and encouraging responsible innovation, the islands can build ecosystems that thrive not just in the short term but for years to come.

The Global Context

The experiences of Puerto Rico and the Bahamas reflect broader trends in how jurisdictions compete to attract crypto business. Their success or failure will offer valuable lessons for other regions seeking to navigate the complex intersection of technology, finance, and regulation.

As pioneers in this space, they have the opportunity to set precedents, establish models, and contribute to shaping the global landscape of digital assets.

Charting the Course to Paradise

The allure of creating a "crypto paradise" is strong, but the journey requires careful navigation. Puerto Rico and the Bahamas stand at the forefront of this exciting yet challenging frontier.

By embracing innovation with eyes wide open to the risks, implementing thoughtful regulations, and fostering inclusive communities, they can turn the vision of a tropical haven for crypto into a sustainable reality.

In doing so, they not only enhance their own economies but also contribute to the evolution of the global financial system—a system that, much like the islands themselves, must be resilient, adaptable, and ever-attuned to the winds of change.

Chapter 18: Putin's People and the Art of Dodging Sanctions

In the grand theater of global politics, sanctions are the West's weapon of choice—a financial equivalent of a stern finger wagging. But for those well-versed in the shadows, like **Vladimir Putin** and his inner circle, sanctions are less of a blockade and more of an inconvenient speed bump on the road to... wherever they please.

A Masterclass in Financial Hide-and-Seek

Long before "sanctions evasion" became cocktail party chatter, Putin was honing his craft in the fine art of financial subterfuge. Back in his **KGB** days in Dresden, he didn't just sip the local brew; he absorbed the East German knack for operating in the gray areas of finance. **Shell companies?** Check. **Offshore accounts?** Double-check. Secretive banking structures that would make a spy novelist raise an eyebrow? You bet.

Fast forward to today, and those early lessons have blossomed into a full-fledged playbook. When Western nations started slapping sanctions on Russia like stickers on a tourist's overstuffed suitcase, Putin's People[16] didn't panic. They simply dusted off their

---

[16] https://amzn.to/40xdAB0

old strategies, added a dash of modern tech, and carried on as if nothing had happened.

Crypto: The New Swiss Bank Account

Enter **cryptocurrency**, the digital darling of rebels and financiers alike. For Russia's elite, crypto isn't just about riding the Bitcoin rollercoaster; it's a lifeline. **Stablecoins** like Tether became the go-to for moving wealth swiftly and, more importantly, discreetly. After all, when your assets are frozen and your yachts are being seized faster than you can say "oligarch," alternative methods are a must.

Why bother with traditional banks—those stuffy institutions that inconveniently follow international law—when you can transfer millions with a few clicks and a knowing wink to the blockchain? Crypto exchanges saw a surge in Russian activity, as rubles were swapped for digital assets that didn't come with strings attached.

BRICS+: The New Kids on the Financial Block

But why stop at crypto when you can redesign the entire playground? Russia, along with its **BRICS buddies**—Brazil, India, China, and South Africa—started chatting about creating their own financial sandbox. Imagine a **BRICS stablecoin**, immune to Western sanctions and **SWIFT** rejections. It's like starting a club where you make the rules, and the old bouncers can't kick you out.

This wasn't just financial maneuvering; it was a geopolitical chess move. By strengthening ties with nations willing to sidestep Western influence, Russia aimed to keep its economy humming and its elite comfortable. Barter deals, local currency trades, and crypto payments became the new normal in this alternative financial universe.

Wagner Group: The Shadow Army with a Shadow Budget

No discussion of Putin's financial acrobatics would be complete without mentioning the **Wagner Group**—a private military company that operates where official forces prefer not to tread. Funding such an outfit requires creativity, especially under sanctions.

Shadow banking and crypto transactions provided the financial lifeblood for Wagner's far-flung operations. From conflict zones to resource-rich regions, they moved with the stealth of a cat and the funding of a small nation. It's a reminder that in the complex game of modern geopolitics, not all battles are fought openly—or funded transparently.

Putin and the "Misplaced Childhood" of the Russian Economy

Russia's ability to sidestep sanctions isn't just a testament to its ingenuity; it's a spotlight on the challenges of enforcing financial restrictions in a digital, interconnected world. For every door that sanctions close, a window—or perhaps a blockchain node—opens.

For global regulators, it's like playing **Whac-A-Mole** with a blindfold on. As soon as one channel is shut down, another pops up. And while sanctions may slow things down, they haven't stopped the flow—at least not yet.

The takeaway? In the grand cat-and-mouse chase of international finance, the mice have gotten smarter, and the cat needs a tech upgrade.

In the sprawling narrative of global economics, Russia is that prodigious child who aced the entrance exam but somehow got lost on the way to class. Under President Vladimir Putin, the Russian economy has been a perplexing blend of untapped potential and questionable priorities—a "misplaced childhood" marked by missed opportunities, an overbearing guardian, and a fixation on playing with the shiniest toys.

The Resource Trap: When Blessings Become Chains

Russia sits atop a treasure trove of natural resources that would make a pirate reconsider his career choices. With vast reserves of oil and gas, it's as if Mother Nature decided to store all her energy drinks in one place. This abundance should have been the springboard to a diversified, robust economy. Instead, it became a comfortable couch from which Russia saw little reason to move.

The reliance on resource extraction turned into a classic case of the **"resource curse."** High revenues from oil and gas exports created a complacency that stifled innovation. Why invest in tech startups or manufacturing when you can just drill another hole and watch the petrodollars gush out? It's like a student who, after inheriting a fortune, decides that studying is for suckers.

But as any economist worth their salt will tell you, overdependence on commodities is a precarious game. Commodity prices fluctuate more than a teenager's mood, and when they dip, so does the national fortune. Diversification isn't just a buzzword; it's the financial equivalent of not putting all your eggs in one barrel of crude oil.

The Control Complex: Big Brother Meets Big Business

Under Putin's tenure, the Russian government developed a penchant for control that would make a helicopter parent look laissez-faire. Key industries didn't just get regulated; they got enveloped, with the state asserting dominance over energy, media, and more. Private initiative became the economic equivalent of an endangered species.

This stranglehold on sectors stifled competition and innovation. Entrepreneurs found themselves navigating a maze of bureaucracy and political gatekeeping that would make Kafka nod in recognition. Barriers to entry weren't just high; they were guarded by metaphorical (and sometimes literal) bears.

Small and medium-sized enterprises (SMEs) struggled to gain traction in an environment where the rules could change overnight, often without warning. It's hard to plan a business strategy when you're constantly looking over your shoulder, wondering if today's the day your industry becomes "of national interest" and subject to government acquisition.

Misplaced Priorities: Tanks Over Textbooks

One might think that a nation with Russia's resources would invest heavily in education, healthcare, and infrastructure—the holy trinity of sustainable economic development. But instead, the Kremlin seemed more interested in a different trinity: military spending, geopolitical chess games, and grandiose projects of questionable utility.

Military parades showcasing the latest hardware became regular spectacles, while schools and hospitals languished. Infrastructure projects were often more about prestige than practicality—a bridge to nowhere here, a lavish stadium there. It's akin to a family spending its savings on a flashy new car while the roof leaks and the kids need new shoes.

This misallocation of resources not only hampered the development of human capital but also sent a clear message about national priorities. When the government invests more in missiles than in microscopes, scientists and innovators take the hint—and sometimes, the next flight out.

The Brain Drain: When the Best and Brightest Pack Their Bags

Russia boasts a highly educated population with a rich tradition in science, literature, and the arts. Yet, the combination of limited opportunities, stifling bureaucracy, and a political climate that frowns upon dissent has led to a mass exodus of talent.

Engineers, doctors, artists, and entrepreneurs have sought greener pastures where their skills are rewarded, and their voices heard. This brain drain is more than a loss of individual talent; it's a hemorrhaging of the very lifeblood that could rejuvenate the Russian economy.

The cycle is self-perpetuating. As more talented individuals leave, innovation declines, making the economy less dynamic and further discouraging those who remain. It's a downward spiral reminiscent of a sinking ship where the crew decides to abandon rather than bail water.

The Path Not Taken: A Study in "What If?"

Imagine, if you will, a Russia that leveraged its vast resources not as a crutch but as a catalyst. A nation that invested in technology, encouraged entrepreneurship, and fostered a climate where innovation thrived alongside tradition. The potential was—and perhaps still is—staggering.

With its educated populace and cultural richness, Russia could have positioned itself as a global leader in various industries beyond energy—technology, pharmaceuticals, renewable energy, to name a few. Instead, the focus remained on consolidating power and projecting strength through traditional means.

The opportunity cost is immeasurable. While other nations embraced globalization and technological advancement, Russia seemed content to play an outdated game, missing out on the collaborative and economic benefits that come with being a proactive member of the global community.

Reclaiming the Future

The "misplaced childhood" of the Russian economy is a narrative filled with ironies and missed cues. A country endowed with every advantage chose a path that limited its own potential, prioritizing control over creativity and short-term gains over long-term prosperity.

But all is not lost. Recognizing the missteps is the first stride toward correction. By shifting priorities—investing in people, embracing innovation, and opening up to genuine competition—Russia can still chart a new course.

The challenges are significant, but so is the resilience ingrained in Russian history and culture. It requires a willingness to let go of old paradigms, to trust in the ingenuity of its people, and to engage with the world not as a wary adversary but as a collaborative partner.

In doing so, Russia can move beyond its prolonged adolescence into a mature economy that reflects its true potential—a place where the prodigious child not only finds the classroom but graduates with honors.

Chapter 19: The Wagner Group—Mercenaries Without Borders

In the shadowy realm of modern warfare, where deniability is as coveted as firepower, the **Wagner Group** stands out as a particularly enigmatic player. Often described as a private military company (PMC), Wagner operates in the gray areas between official state action and independent mercenary work, leaving a trail of geopolitical intrigue and ethical quandaries in its wake.

Origins: The Birth of a Shadow Army

The Wagner Group emerged in the early 2010s, reportedly founded by **Dmitry Utkin**, a former lieutenant colonel in Russia's military intelligence agency, the **GRU**. Utkin, whose alleged fascination with the Third Reich inspired the group's name—after Richard Wagner, Hitler's favored composer—assembled a force capable of projecting Russian interests abroad while providing plausible deniability to the Kremlin.

Officially, the Russian government denies any connection to Wagner. Unofficially, the group's activities often align so closely with Russia's foreign policy objectives that the line between state and private action becomes almost indistinguishable. It's like claiming your right hand doesn't know what the left is doing, even though they're clapping in perfect unison.

Operations: From Ukraine to Syria and Beyond

Wagner's mercenaries have appeared in conflict zones across the globe, including **Ukraine**, **Syria**, **Libya**, the **Central African Republic**, and **Mali**. In each theater, they serve as force multipliers for local allies, trainers for military forces, or direct combatants against adversaries.

In Ukraine, they first surfaced during the annexation of **Crimea** and the conflict in Eastern Ukraine, providing support to separatist forces. In Syria, Wagner fighters bolstered the **Assad regime**, engaging in some of the most intense battles of the civil war. Their deployment often coincides with regions where Russia has strategic interests, such as access to resources or geopolitical influence.

A Business Model Built on Conflict

Wagner's operations are not purely altruistic—or even purely political. The group reportedly secures lucrative contracts for resource extraction in exchange for military support. In Syria, for example, Wagner-linked entities were said to have secured oil and gas rights. In Africa, they've been involved in mining operations for valuable minerals.

It's a business model that monetizes conflict: provide the muscle to tip the scales in a client's favor, and reap the rewards through access to natural resources. It's capitalism meeting militarism in a fusion that's as profitable as it is ethically murky.

Human Rights Concerns: The Dark Side of Denial

Wherever Wagner operates, allegations of human rights abuses often follow. Reports have surfaced of extrajudicial killings, torture, and indiscriminate violence against civilians. In the Central African Republic, journalists investigating Wagner's activities were mysteriously killed, raising suspicions about the group's methods of handling scrutiny.

The lack of official acknowledgment from the Russian government complicates efforts to hold Wagner accountable. If a PMC doesn't officially exist, how do you prosecute its crimes? It's the international relations equivalent of fighting a ghost.

Geopolitics: Deniable Assets in Global Chess

For the Kremlin, Wagner provides a valuable tool: the ability to exert influence without the political fallout of deploying official military forces. If things go well, Russia gains strategic advantages. If things go poorly, they can distance themselves from any failures or atrocities.

This deniability strains international norms and challenges the traditional understanding of state responsibility. It introduces new complexities into global diplomacy, where non-state actors wield significant military power but operate outside conventional legal frameworks.

The Business of War in the 21st Century

The Wagner Group exemplifies the evolving nature of conflict in our modern era. They blur the lines between state and private interests, between soldier and mercenary, between war and commerce. Their rise forces us to confront uncomfortable questions about accountability, ethics, and the future of warfare.

As conflicts continue to simmer and geopolitical tensions escalate, entities like Wagner will likely remain fixtures on the global stage. They operate in the shadows, but their impact is as real and devastating as any conventional army.

In the end, the business of death is more than just a grim tagline—it's a profitable enterprise that thrives in the gaps of international law and exploits the ambiguities of modern geopolitics. Addressing the challenges posed by groups like Wagner will require a concerted effort from the international community, one that shines a light into the shadows where they operate.

Jan Marsalek: The Phantom Financier

Speaking of shadows, few figures embody the intrigue of clandestine operations quite like **Jan Marsalek**, the former COO of the now-infamous **Wirecard**. Marsalek's tracks lead into a world that feels at times like a poorly lit B-movie and at others like a plunge into the pages of a spy thriller.

After Wirecard's dramatic collapse—marked by a €1.9 billion hole in its accounts and allegations of widespread fraud—Marsalek vanished, leaving behind a trail of unanswered questions and international arrest warrants. Reports suggest that he had connections with Russian intelligence agencies and that he may have assisted the Wagner Group in their activities, particularly in Africa.

A Journey Through the Looking Glass

Marsalek's fascination with espionage and military operations wasn't just a hobby—it was a lifestyle. He reportedly took trips to war-torn regions, engaged with mercenaries, and even dabbled in arms dealing. One anecdote describes him sitting in the cockpit of a MiG-29 fighter jet, giving a thumbs-up while wearing a pilot's helmet and oxygen mask—a "Top Gun" fever dream come to life.

Associates recall his tales of firing rocket-propelled grenades in Syria and mingling with individuals linked to Russian military intelligence. Whether these stories are the embellishments of an adrenaline junkie or the breadcrumbs of a deeper involvement remains a subject of speculation.

The Wirecard Connection: A Conduit for Cloak-and-Dagger Dealings

Why would Moscow be interested in recruiting Marsalek? As Wirecard's COO, he was in a prime position to facilitate complex financial transactions that could fly under the radar. Wirecard's global payment infrastructure and opaque third-party partnerships provided an ideal platform for moving funds discreetly—potentially useful for intelligence operations or financing groups like Wagner.

There are allegations that Marsalek may have helped transfer money to Russian intelligence agencies and even facilitated payments to Wagner operatives. While these claims remain unverified, they paint a picture of a man deeply entwined in a web of financial and geopolitical intrigue.

A Puppet Master or a Pawn?

Was Marsalek a cunning architect of clandestine operations or merely a tool in a larger game? His interactions with figures linked to Russian intelligence suggest a level of involvement that goes beyond casual acquaintance. Yet, some argue he was manipulated by seasoned operatives who exploited his ambitions and vulnerabilities.

One thing is certain: Marsalek's story underscores the blurred lines between corporate malfeasance and international espionage. It's a tale where boardroom dealings intersect with battlefield maneuvers, and where the pursuit of profit becomes entangled with the shadowy objectives of statecraft.

The Global Implications: Shadows Cast Long

The intertwining of Marsalek's financial acumen with the Wagner Group's military exploits highlights a troubling nexus between illicit finance and armed conflict. It raises pressing questions about the effectiveness of international regulations in preventing money laundering, sanctions evasion, and the funding of unauthorized military activities.

As we navigate an increasingly interconnected world, the actions of individuals like Marsalek and entities like Wagner remind us that the boundaries of legality and morality are often tested in the pursuit of power and profit.

Unmasking the Mercenaries

The Wagner Group and figures like Jan Marsalek exemplify the complexities of modern geopolitics, where non-state actors wield significant influence and where financial systems can be manipulated to serve opaque agendas. They operate in the shadows, but their actions have real-world consequences that ripple across borders and impact global stability.

Addressing these challenges requires more than just policy adjustments—it demands a concerted international effort to enhance transparency, enforce accountability, and reaffirm the principles that underpin the rule of law.

Because in a world where mercenaries without borders can alter the course of nations, shining a light into the shadows isn't just an option—it's an imperative.

Chapter 20: Alexei Navalny—Patriotism with AML

In the grand narrative of modern Russia, few characters are as compelling—or as polarizing—as **Alexei Navalny [PATRIOT**[17]**]**. Imagine a lawyer who looked at the gilded towers of Moscow's elite, rubbed his hands together, and said, "Let's see what's behind door number one." Spoiler alert: It wasn't sunshine and rainbows.

---

[17] https://amzn.to/3UAvUoN

From Legal Eagle to Political Hawk

Navalny started where many ambitious Russians do—in the hallowed halls of law. But instead of climbing the corporate ladder to a corner office with a view of the Kremlin, he decided to kick that ladder over and build his own. Armed with legal expertise and a knack for oratory, he transformed into the Kremlin's most persistent thorn.

Through his **Anti-Corruption Foundation (FBK)**, Navalny [Beautiful Russia's Chief Believer[18]] didn't just ruffle feathers; he plucked the whole chicken. Exposing fraudulent schemes, dubious asset holdings, and embezzlement that would make a pirate blush, he shone a light on the shadowy dealings of Russia's upper echelons. It's as if he took the phrase "sunlight is the best disinfectant" a bit too literally.

In 2012, Navalny unveiled the **"Navalny Card"** [One startup that I regret not having done 10 years ago[19]] —an AML-first digital banking tool designed to bring transparency to Russia's murky financial waters. Think of it as a beacon in a foggy harbor, guiding ships away from the jagged rocks of corruption.

The Navalny Card: Banking on Integrity

The card wasn't just a piece of plastic; it was a statement. In a nation where shadow banking is as common as nesting dolls, introducing a transparent financial instrument was revolutionary. It was like opening a vegan café in a town obsessed with steak— bold, intriguing, and bound to raise eyebrows.

Unfortunately, the Navalny Card [NavalnyCard.ru [rus, 2012][20]] faced hurdles that even the best high jumper couldn't clear. Regulatory

---

[18] https://medium.com/@slavasolodkiy_67243/beautiful-russias-chief-believer-f4e97df685b2

[19] https://medium.com/@slavasolodkiy_67243/one-startup-that-i-regret-not-having-done-10-years-ago-d487002c5937

[20] https://www.slideshare.net/slideshow/navalnycardru-rus-2012/266265222

pressures, lack of institutional support, and the ever-watchful eye of those who preferred the status quo kept the project from reaching its full potential. But the seed was planted, and the conversation about ethical banking in high-risk regions began to sprout.

Navalny's ingenuity extended beyond investigations. The **"Navalny Card"** [One startup that I regret not having done: Navalny Card[21]] was more than a fundraising tool; it was a symbol of transparency and trust. By providing supporters with a means to contribute that was both secure and accountable, he fostered a community bound by shared values.

The "Smart Voting" initiative showcased his strategic acumen. By urging voters to support the most viable opposition candidates, regardless of party affiliation, Navalny sought to break the monopoly of the ruling party through tactical collaboration. It was a masterstroke of political judo, using the system's weight against itself.

The High Cost of High Principles

Navalny's crusade wasn't without peril. In August 2020, he fell gravely ill—later confirmed to be poisoning with **Novichok**, a nerve agent that isn't exactly sold over the counter. While fingers pointed in predictable directions, official narratives twisted themselves into knots trying to explain it away.

Miraculously, Navalny survived and, displaying a level of fortitude that would make Rocky Balboa nod in respect, returned to Russia in January 2021. Upon arrival, he was promptly detained—because nothing says "welcome home" like handcuffs and a courtroom.

His imprisonment transformed him from a mere opposition figure into a symbol—a living testament to the costs of dissent in a

---

[21] https://www.linkedin.com/pulse/one-startup-i-regret-having-done-10-years-ago-vladislav-solodkiy-td1ke/

system that doesn't take kindly to being questioned. From his cell, he continues to inspire, his voice echoing far beyond the prison walls, much to the chagrin of those who put him there.

Patriotism in the Face of Adversity

Navalny's actions stem from a profound sense of patriotism. Not the flag-waving, anthem-singing variety, but a deep-rooted desire to see his country rise above the quagmire of corruption. He isn't just fighting against something; he's fighting for something—a Russia where transparency isn't a novelty and where power isn't a license to plunder. [Navalny's Utopia for Realists[22]]

His story serves as a stark reminder that compliance and transparency aren't just corporate buzzwords; they're pillars of a just society. In regions where shadow banking operates with impunity, standing up for ethical finance is both a daring act and a necessary one.

The Echo of Integrity

Navalny's journey underscores the intersection of finance, politics, and personal conviction. His willingness to challenge entrenched systems at great personal risk elevates the discourse on compliance from mere regulation to moral imperative.

For those in the financial world, his legacy is a call to action. Compliance isn't just about avoiding fines or pleasing regulators; it's about upholding principles that sustain the very fabric of society.

In the end, Navalny reminds us that patriotism isn't measured by unquestioning loyalty, but by the courage to hold one's nation to its highest ideals—even when the cost is steep.

In the annals of modern activism, **Alexei Navalny** stands out as a figure who dared to challenge a formidable system, wielding

---

22 https://www.linkedin.com/pulse/navalnys-utopia-realists-vladislav-solodkiy-kpz1e/

transparency and accountability as his weapons of choice. A lawyer by training and an anti-corruption campaigner by calling, Navalny became a beacon for those yearning to lift the veil on opaque practices and hold power to account.

The Rise of a Relentless Advocate

Navalny didn't just criticize corruption; he dissected it with the precision of a surgeon. Through his **Anti-Corruption Foundation (FBK)**, he launched investigations into the wealth and dealings of Russia's elite, producing detailed reports and documentaries that laid bare the extent of malfeasance.

His approach was methodical and fearless. By targeting high-profile figures and exposing lavish properties, hidden assets, and complex financial webs, Navalny struck at the very heart of entrenched corruption. It was compliance activism on a grand scale, shining a light into the darkest corners.

Harnessing Technology: The Digital Sword

Recognizing the power of technology [How To Build Government-In-The-Cloud or Country-As-A-Service?[23]], Navalny leveraged social media, blogs, and video platforms to disseminate his findings. This digital strategy bypassed traditional media channels, many of which were state-controlled or influenced, reaching millions of Russians directly.

His team employed **open-source intelligence (OSINT)** techniques [From Dissident to Detective: On the Way to ShmagunGPT[24]], sifting through public records, satellite images, and data leaks to piece together the puzzle of corruption. It was citizen auditing at its finest, turning the tools of the information age into instruments of accountability.

---

[23] https://www.slideshare.net/slideshow/initial-country-offering-how-to-build-governmentinthecloud-or-countryasaservice/85282076

[24] https://medium.com/@slavasolodkiy_67243/from-dissident-to-detective-on-the-way-to-shmagungpt-6bcf05c3fbba

Navalny's journey was fraught with peril. From legal harassment to imprisonment, he faced immense personal risks. Yet, his resolve remained unshaken. His willingness to stand up, even when the cost was high, underscores the profound impact one individual can have in challenging systemic issues.

The Compliance Crusader's Legacy: Inspiring a New Generation

Navalny's relentless pursuit of transparency wasn't just about exposing corruption; it was about empowering others to demand better. He demonstrated that compliance isn't a box-ticking exercise confined to corporate boardrooms but a societal imperative that affects every citizen.

His work has had a ripple effect, inspiring activists worldwide to embrace technology, innovation, and unwavering integrity in the fight against corruption. By melding legal expertise with cutting-edge tactics, Navalny redefined what it means to be a compliance crusader in the 21st century.

Alexei Navalny's story is a testament to the power of conviction and the impact of innovative approaches to age-old problems [The Ironic Protagonist: Believers and Betrayers[25]]. His legacy serves as a clarion call to individuals and institutions alike: that transparency, accountability, and ethical conduct are not mere ideals but actionable principles that can reshape societies.

In a world where compliance often conjures images of dense regulations and bureaucratic hurdles, Navalny breathed life into the concept, showing that at its core, compliance is about justice, fairness, and the courage to speak truth to power.

As we reflect on his contributions, we are reminded that the pursuit of a more transparent and accountable world is a shared responsibility. Whether through technology, activism, or everyday

---

[25] https://www.linkedin.com/pulse/ironic-protagonist-believers-betrayers-vladislav-solodkiy-nyzie/

choices, each of us has a role to play in upholding the standards that Navalny so passionately championed.

His journey inspires us to look beyond the confines of our roles and consider the broader impact of our actions. In doing so, we honor not just his legacy but the enduring quest for integrity in all facets of life.

Chapter 21: Trump and the "Art of the (Compliance) Deal"

In the grand theater of global business, few names have commanded as much spotlight as **Donald J. Trump** [Donald Trump, Russian money & (Anti) Money Laundering[26]] and his eponymous **Trump Organization**. A real estate empire adorned with gilded towers, opulent hotels, and golf courses that promise luxury with every swing, the Trump Organization is as much a brand as it is a business. Yet, behind the shimmering facades and bold typography lies a labyrinth of complex transactions, international dealings, and a fair share of controversies.

The Trump Organization's business model is a tapestry of ventures that span the globe. From skyscrapers in Manhattan to resorts in Scotland, its reach is both wide and deep. The company's penchant for licensing deals, where the Trump name adorns properties owned and operated by others, adds another layer of complexity to its operations.

The Trump Organization's High-Stakes Game

This global footprint naturally brings with it a host of compliance challenges. Operating across multiple jurisdictions means navigating a maze of regulations, each with its own quirks and demands. Add to this the high-profile nature of the brand, and the

---

[26] https://www.slideshare.net/slideshow/donald-trump-russian-money-anti-money-laundering/272942303

scrutiny intensifies. It's a bit like juggling flaming torches while walking a tightrope—over a pit of regulatory alligators.

Over the years, the Trump Organization has faced various allegations related to financial misconduct. Critics and investigative journalists have raised questions about everything from tax strategies to the sourcing of investment funds. Some have pointed to the complex ownership structures and partnerships with foreign entities as potential red flags requiring closer examination.

It's important to note that allegations are not convictions, and suspicions are not evidence. In the world of high finance and real estate, especially on an international scale, complexity is par for the course. However, complexity can sometimes obscure clarity, making it all the more vital for organizations to maintain robust compliance practices.

Compliance in the Spotlight

The Trump Organization's experiences highlight the critical importance of compliance, especially for businesses operating on a global stage. Robust **KYC (Know Your Customer)** and **AML (Anti-Money Laundering)** procedures are not just regulatory requirements but essential tools for risk management. Transparency in transactions, clear ownership structures, and meticulous record-keeping are the bedrock of sound business practices.

For companies like the Trump Organization, the intersection of business and politics adds another layer of complexity. Political exposure can amplify risks and attract additional scrutiny from regulators and the public alike. This makes a strong compliance culture not just advisable but indispensable.

The Pursuit of Transparency

In an era where public trust is both fragile and invaluable, the ability of organizations to demonstrate transparency and accountability is paramount. Independent audits, third-party assessments, and a willingness to engage openly with regulatory bodies can go a long way in building and maintaining that trust.

The challenges faced by the Trump Organization serve as a case study for businesses worldwide. They underscore the need for proactive compliance measures and the dangers of complacency in an increasingly interconnected and regulated world.

Lessons for the Modern Enterprise

The story of the Trump Organization is multifaceted, reflecting the complexities of global business in the 21st century. While allegations and controversies may swirl, the underlying lesson is clear: compliance is not merely a bureaucratic hurdle but a strategic imperative.

Businesses must navigate not only market forces but also the evolving expectations of regulators, investors, and the public. By prioritizing transparency, ethical practices, and robust compliance systems, organizations can better position themselves for sustainable success—avoiding pitfalls that can tarnish reputations and erode trust.

In the art of the deal, as in the art of compliance, attention to detail, integrity, and foresight are the keys to mastering the canvas.

Chapter 22: The Hijacking —When Compliance Met Compromise

The transition from visionary founder to sidelined minority shareholder is a plot twist no entrepreneur wants to experience. Yet, that's precisely the drama that unfolded at **ArivalBank.com**. Just as we were solidifying our reputation as a compliance fortress for the financially misunderstood, unforeseen forces began to reshape our carefully constructed edifice.

The Changing Tide: From Majority to Minority

In the startup world, securing investment is akin to walking a tightrope—you need the funds to grow, but you risk losing your balance if the investors don't share your vision. As ArivalBank.com gained traction, we attracted the attention of investors with deep pockets and grand ambitions. Initially, this seemed like the perfect marriage of resources and innovation.

But as the ink dried on the contracts, it became apparent that our new partners had different priorities. They weren't just investing in ArivalBank.com; they were intent on steering the ship. Suddenly, the captain's chair felt more like a ceremonial throne, with real decisions being made in backrooms where compliance was viewed more as a hurdle than a hallmark.

A Clash of Cultures: Integrity vs. Expediency

Our commitment to rigorous compliance wasn't just a business strategy—it was a core value. However, the new majority shareholders saw compliance as an expensive speed bump on the fast lane to profitability. They pushed for rapid expansion into markets and client segments that raised red flags—both ethically and legally.

Discussions about onboarding clients with opaque backgrounds became more frequent. Suggestions to "streamline" due diligence processes were thinly veiled attempts to cut corners. It was like watching someone dismantle the very foundation of the house to speed up renovations.

The Geopolitical Storm: Shadows on the Horizon

Complicating matters further, global events were reshaping the financial landscape. The invasion of Ukraine sent shockwaves through international markets. Sanctions were imposed, and the scrutiny on financial transactions involving certain regions intensified.

Ironically, as the world tightened its regulatory grip, there was a surge in demand for high-risk and shadow banking services. Institutions and individuals seeking to bypass sanctions began looking for channels to move their funds—a risky business that we had meticulously avoided.

The new leadership at ArivalBank.com, however, seemed less deterred by these risks. The allure of quick profits overshadowed the potential legal and reputational consequences. It was as if we had built a fortress to keep out the wolves, only to have someone open the gates from the inside.

Personal Convictions and Professional Consequences

Around this tumultuous time, I made a personal decision that would further strain my relationship with the new management. Inspired by a commitment to transparency and anti-corruption, I chose to support organizations advocating for these values. This included expressing support for figures like **Alexei Navalny** and his **Anti-Corruption Foundation**.

In an environment where political alliances and business interests are often intertwined, this was a contentious move. My stance on these issues didn't align with the objectives—or perhaps the comfort zones—of the new majority shareholders. The tension was palpable, and it wasn't long before it escalated into actions that effectively marginalized me within the company I had built.

The Inevitable Ousting: When Founder Becomes Outsider

Decisions were made without my input. Access to information was restricted. It became clear that my role was being minimized, and my influence diminished. The very ethos of compliance and integrity that had defined ArivalBank.com was being eroded from within.

Watching this unfold was like witnessing a carefully nurtured garden being overrun by weeds. The frustration was immense, but so was the realization that staying on board would mean compromising on principles that were non-negotiable.

Reflections on Control and Consequences

This experience underscored a harsh reality in the world of business: the vision that starts a company isn't always the one that sees it through. Control isn't just about ownership percentages; it's about aligning values and ensuring that all stakeholders are committed to the same ethical standards.

The takeover of ArivalBank.com was more than a corporate restructuring; it was a pivot away from the principles that had been our guiding stars. The emphasis shifted from responsible innovation to opportunistic expansion, from meticulous compliance to calculated risk-taking.

The Aftermath: Lessons Etched in Experience

While the loss of control over ArivalBank.com was disheartening, it provided invaluable lessons. It highlighted the importance of choosing investors and partners who share not just the business goals but also the ethical framework.

It also reinforced the belief that compliance and integrity are not just boxes to tick but are foundational to sustainable success. In an industry fraught with risks and the temptation to cut corners, holding steadfast to one's principles isn't just honorable—it's essential.

The chapter with ArivalBank.com may have closed, but the story doesn't end there. Armed with the lessons learned and an unwavering commitment to ethical banking, the journey continues. There's a renewed focus on building ventures that prioritize transparency, integrity, and innovation without compromise.

Because at the end of the day, while control over a company can be taken away, control over one's values and principles remains firmly in one's own hands.

Chapter 23: Wirecard's Ghost: Has Singapore Learned its Lesson?

Singapore, the gleaming city-state known for its impeccable cleanliness, efficient governance, and economic prowess, stands as a beacon of modernity in Asia. Its skyline is dotted with architectural marvels, its ports teem with activity, and its financial district buzzes with the hum of global commerce. Yet, beneath this polished exterior lies a complex challenge: maintaining its status as a global financial hub while guarding against the murky waters of shadow banking.

A Financial Powerhouse

Singapore's rise as a financial center is no accident. Strategic location, pro-business policies, strong rule of law, and a reputation for stability have attracted banks, investment firms, and multinational corporations from around the world. The Monetary Authority of Singapore (MAS), the country's central bank and financial regulator, is lauded for its prudent oversight and progressive approach.

The nation's commitment to innovation is evident in its embrace of fintech, digital banking, and blockchain technologies. Regulatory sandboxes encourage experimentation while maintaining safeguards—a delicate balance that fuels growth without sacrificing security.

The Shadows Cast by Success

However, the very attributes that make Singapore attractive to legitimate businesses can also appeal to less scrupulous actors.

The ease of doing business, sophisticated financial infrastructure, and connectivity to global markets can be exploited for illicit purposes if not carefully monitored.

Shadow banking—financial activities that occur outside traditional banking regulations—poses a risk. This includes unregulated lending, opaque investment vehicles, and complex transactions that can obscure the origins and destinations of funds.

Regulatory Vigilance: The Unseen Guardians

Singapore's authorities are acutely aware of these risks. MAS and other agencies have implemented stringent measures to combat money laundering, terrorism financing, and other financial crimes. Know Your Customer (KYC) protocols, Suspicious Transaction Reports (STRs), and collaboration with international bodies are integral parts of the defense.

The challenge lies in staying ahead of increasingly sophisticated schemes. As financial products become more complex and technology enables rapid movement of funds, regulators must continually adapt. It's a high-stakes game of cat and mouse, with significant implications for the integrity of the financial system.

Striving for Transparency

Transparency is a key weapon against shadow banking. By promoting open reporting standards, enhancing disclosure requirements, and encouraging ethical practices, Singapore aims to make the shadows less accommodating for illicit activities.

Initiatives like the Anti-Money Laundering and Countering the Financing of Terrorism Industry Partnership (ACIP) bring together public and private sectors to share insights and develop strategies. Such collaboration enhances the collective ability to detect and deter wrongdoing.

Innovation with Caution

Singapore's pursuit of innovation is tempered with caution. Regulatory frameworks are designed to foster growth while imposing necessary controls. For example, the licensing of digital banks comes with rigorous assessments to ensure that new entrants meet standards of governance and risk management.

The country's approach serves as a model for how to embrace technological advancement without opening doors to exploitation. By setting clear expectations and maintaining oversight, Singapore demonstrates that progress and protection can coexist.

Navigating the Crossroads

Singapore's position at the crossroads of global finance brings both opportunities and responsibilities. As it continues to shine as a hub of commerce and innovation, the vigilance against shadow banking must remain unwavering.

By upholding principles of transparency, accountability, and robust regulation, Singapore can mitigate risks while capitalizing on its strengths. The journey requires constant adaptation and a commitment to integrity—a path that, if navigated wisely, will ensure that the Lion City roars with prosperity without casting unintended shadows.

Epilogue: Metaverse Compliance Officer

As we close this book, we find ourselves at a crossroads—not unlike the characters in our story. Do we continue to play by the old rules, knowing their limitations, or do we dare to imagine a new paradigm? One where compliance isn't just about ticking boxes but about fostering a culture of transparency and accountability. One where dreamers and realists find common ground in their pursuit of a better future.

In the grand tapestry of global finance and politics, where compliance officers are the unsung heroes and anti-money laundering efforts are the quiet battles waged in the shadows, there lies a story—a story of utopia, of believers and betrayers, of dreamers who dared to envision… a 'beautiful Russia'.

Russians Everywhere

Imagine a modern-day political drama unfolding in the heart of Moscow, reminiscent of "The Crown's" regal intrigue and "House of Cards'" Machiavellian maneuvers, sprinkled with the satirical wit of "Freakonomics." Our protagonist is none other than **Alexei Navalny**, the audacious anti-corruption crusader, the chief believer in a realist's utopia.

Navalny, armed not with weapons but with wit, irony, and an unyielding commitment to exposing corruption, becomes the embodiment of hope for a Russia that might yet be. His journey is a testament to the power of resilience and the audacity of believing in change, even when the odds are stacked higher than the Kremlin walls.

In the shadows, the ever-present figure of **Vladimir Putin** looms— a master of political sambo, deftly exploiting the weaknesses of both his adversaries and the hesitant West. His ascent from a modest KGB agent in Dresden to the helm of Russian power is a narrative woven with threads of calculated strategy and an understanding of the darker arts of governance. He's the antagonist who doesn't just play the game but rewrites the rules mid-match.

But this isn't just a Russian story—it's a global one. The echoes of **Ukraine's** resilience under leaders like **Volodymyr Zelensky** reverberate throughout, highlighting parallel narratives of nations grappling with identity and defying the gravitational pull of authoritarianism. Zelensky's rise from comedian to president is the kind of plot twist that makes reality seem stranger than fiction—a reminder that sometimes, life imitates art in the most unexpected ways.

In this imagined future, Navalny's vision transcends borders—both physical and digital. The concept of the **"Navalny Card,"** once an anti-corruption initiative, evolves into the **"Digital Nansen Passport,"** offering exiled Russians and Belarusians a new kind of citizenship rooted not in geography but in shared values and aspirations. It's a bold idea that would make even the most seasoned compliance officers raise an eyebrow and perhaps, secretly, nod in approval.

As this digital nation—the first **metastate**—grows, it challenges traditional notions of sovereignty and governance. It's a decentralized network where blockchain technology ensures transparency—a utopia for realists who understand that to change the system, sometimes you have to rebuild it from the ground up. It's the kind of innovative disruption that keeps regulators awake at night and visionaries dreaming by day.

Of course, no grand narrative is complete without a touch of irony. The West, often paralyzed by its own indecision, watches these developments unfold, perhaps drafting yet another strongly worded statement while sipping imported vodka. Meanwhile, the digital revolution marches on, undeterred by borders or bureaucracy, much like a compliance officer's to-do list—ever-growing and blissfully ignorant of weekends.

In the world of compliance and AML, this story serves as both inspiration and caution. It highlights the relentless ingenuity of those who seek to circumvent the system and the equally relentless pursuit of those who aim to uphold integrity. It's a reminder that in the ever-evolving landscape of global finance and politics, the lines between right and wrong are often as clear as Moscow in a snowstorm. Because, as the tale of the beautiful believers of Russia shows us, utopia might just be achievable—if we're willing to believe, to act, and perhaps most importantly, to inject a bit of irony and intellectual humor along the way.

A Glimpse into the Future – The Age of Automated Integrity

It's the year 2045. The world has changed—on paper, at least. Digital currencies have replaced traditional banknotes, and each citizen has their own "Personal Compliance Rating," courtesy of the Global Integrity Bureau. Society is immaculate, meticulously monitored, and—in theory—free from the corruption and financial chicanery that once plagued the world.

In this polished landscape, algorithms reign supreme, with AI-powered compliance systems managing everything from individual transactions to corporate disclosures. This system doesn't merely verify identities or detect fraud; it does the thinking for us. From the mundane purchase of a coffee to the sale of a global conglomerate, each transaction flows through layers of AI filters designed to ensure absolute purity. The innocent days of "Know Your Customer" are long gone; now, it's "Know Your Intentions, Know Your Past, and Know Your Future Potential." As every citizen walks through life, their digital shadow is always ahead of them, scrutinizing and predicting their next move.

This future of AML and compliance has brought us one thing, though: unparalleled efficiency. There's no need for audits, compliance departments, or regulations. Our lives have become compliant by design. Banks—if they can still be called that—are sleek, sterile places, devoid of the usual charm of a teller's smile or the hopeful glint of a loan officer's eye. Instead, we are greeted by holographic AI consultants, who inform us politely but firmly that our recent purchases indicate "excessive discretionary spending," and advise us on financial moderation.

But this flawless system, for all its precision, has an unintended side effect: a society of strict compliance has become a society of extraordinary predictability. No one invests on a whim; no one takes financial risks. Startups are a thing of the past, with any hint of innovation run through multiple risk filters until all disruptive potential is drained. The entrepreneurs of the past are now replaced by "Certified Innovators," pre-selected by algorithms to ensure they do not deviate from approved business models. The world runs on compliance, but creativity has become a compliance risk.

There's a certain irony to it all, really. The very systems we built to catch rogue bankers, laundered money, and clandestine deals have done their job so well that they've wiped out the human spirit of ambition, defiance, and yes—even the occasional scandal. Compliance now controls society's heartbeat, with the sound of a thousand tiny risk calculations guiding every transaction, every investment, and every decision.

As we close on this world, the question lingers: did we create a safer world—or just a quieter one? And somewhere, in the distant memory of a world less bound by rules, echoes the thought: perhaps a little chaos was necessary, after all.

hugs, **Slava Solodkiy**

https://l.Nansen.ID/Slava

Recommended reading:

- PATRIOT[27]: the Sunday Times bestselling memoir and secret prison diaries by the fearless Russian opposition leader - **by Alexei Navalny**
- Putin's People[28]: A Times Book of the Year 2021 – The Story of Russia's History and Politics - **by Catherine Belton**
- Kleptopia[29]: How Dirty Money is Conquering the World - **by Tom Burgis**
- Money Men[30]: A Hot Startup, A Billion Dollar Fraud, A Fight for the Truth - **by Dan McCrum**

Sources and References:

1. [Digital] Identity is the new money[31]
2. $175 Trillion Problem: Or How to Create the Ultimate Debt Crisis in 12 Easy Steps[32]
3. A Lone Fighter Against the Legal Giants: The Ally in Your Corner for 20$[33]
4. An Online-Court in Singapore, or Justice-as-a-Service: A New Paradigm?[34]
5. Anti-War Russians Face Many Problems, Oligarchs Do Not[35]
6. ArivalBank.com Takeover: A Minority Shareholder's Struggle for Justice[36]
7. Arrival of the compliance-as-a-service[37]
8. Beautiful Russia's Chief Believer[38]

---

[27] https://amzn.to/3UAvUoN

[28] https://amzn.to/40xdAB0

[29] https://amzn.to/4hLfKDl

[30] https://amzn.to/3YxUfNt

[31] https://www.slideshare.net/slideshow/digital-identity-is-the-new-money/100705902

[32] https://www.linkedin.com/pulse/175-trillion-problem-how-create-ultimate-debt-crisis-12-solodkiy-lqiae/

[33] https://medium.com/@slavasolodkiy_67243/a-lone-fighter-against-the-legal-giants-the-ally-in-your-corner-for-20-6c761a3764e5

[34] https://www.linkedin.com/pulse/online-court-singapore-justice-as-a-service-new-vladislav-solodkiy-my6je/

[35] https://www.linkedin.com/pulse/anti-war-russians-face-many-problems-oligarchs-do-vladislav-solodkiy-jeeme/

[36] https://medium.com/@slavasolodkiy_67243/arivalbank-com-takeover-a-minority-shareholders-struggle-for-justice-3d16da5e73ed

[37] https://www.slideshare.net/slideshow/arrival-of-aid-complianceasaservice-solution/174265982

[38] https://medium.com/@slavasolodkiy_67243/beautiful-russias-chief-believer-

---

f4e97df685b2

[39] https://www.slideshare.net/slideshow/banks-and-regulators-in-fintech-results-of-2016-and-trends-for-2017/76789007

[40] https://medium.com/@slavasolodkiy_67243/compliance-demystified-a-beginners-guide-d41342fdc056

[41] https://medium.com/arivalbank/compliance-is-sexy-and-arival-knows-it-3d7094f53131

[42] https://www.slideshare.net/slideshow/correspondent-banking-market-overview/262636406

[43] https://www.slideshare.net/vsolodkiy/cryptorelated-clients-play-cat-and-mouse-with-banks

[44] https://www.slideshare.net/slideshow/donald-trump-russian-money-anti-money-laundering/272942303

[45] https://medium.com/@slavasolodkiy_67243/estonian-experience-for-puerto-rico-what-about-initial-country-offering-for-70b-8cc7e2656a6f

[46] https://www.linkedin.com/pulse/eu-lawmakers-easing-opening-bank-accounts-obtaining-visas-solodkiy-zpc0e/

[47] https://medium.com/@slavasolodkiy_67243/eu-on-easing-the-opening-of-bank-accounts-for-anti-putins-41134cc2a63a

[48] https://www.linkedin.com/pulse/fintech-more-correspondent-banking-still-untouched-niche-solodkiy/

[49] https://podcasters.spotify.com/pod/show/metastate

[50] https://www.slideshare.net/slideshow/followthemoney-brock-pierce-tether-deltec-ftx/272943361

[51] https://www.linkedin.com/pulse/forbes-war-arival-bank-vladislav-solodkiy-bewae/

[52] https://medium.com/@slavasolodkiy_67243/forbes-war-at-arival-bank-54f2f114ad65

[53] https://medium.com/@slavasolodkiy_67243/from-dissident-to-detective-on-the-way-to-shmagungpt-6bcf05c3fbba

[54] https://medium.com/@slavasolodkiy_67243/from-enrc-to-arival-a-pattern-of-behavior-or-just-a-coincidence-b96f30e1b3f8

---

[55] https://www.linkedin.com/pulse/from-enrc-arival-oligarchs-shadow-over-singapore-courts-solodkiy-y0qfe/

[56] https://medium.com/@slavasolodkiy_67243/from-marx-to-balaji-network-states-as-many-dominant-classes-and-no-one-loses-33f2532d73c5

[57] https://www.linkedin.com/pulse/high-risk-compliance-baas-correspondent-banks-vladislav-solodkiy-4eotc/

[58] https://www.linkedin.com/pulse/how-i-took-seven-top-expensive-lawyers-armed-just-chatgpt-solodkiy-ntf5e/

[59] https://www.slideshare.net/slideshow/initial-country-offering-how-to-build-governmentinthecloud-or-countryasaservice/85282076

[60] https://www.linkedin.com/pulse/how-could-world-id-better-least-useful-vladislav-solodkiy-ri4me/

[61] https://www.linkedin.com/pulse/identityinc-72-competitors-worldcoin-vladislav-solodkiy/

[62] https://www.slideshare.net/slideshow/jan-marsalek-from-wirecard-to-putin-s-spy/272942314

[63] https://medium.com/@slavasolodkiy/kaufman-rossin-on-russian-oligarchs-and-sanctions-bb49d9e571f0

[64] https://www.slideshare.net/slideshow/navalnycardru-rus-2012/266265222

[65] https://www.slideshare.net/slideshow/navalnycardru-for-cannes-lions-rus-2012/266265189

[66] https://www.linkedin.com/pulse/navalnys-utopia-realists-vladislav-solodkiy-kpz1e/

[67] https://www.linkedin.com/pulse/nansenid-worldcoin-550-million-people-sanctioned-vladislav-solodkiy-sulce/

[68] https://medium.com/@slavasolodkiy_67243/one-startup-that-i-regret-not-having-done-10-years-ago-d487002c5937

[69] https://www.linkedin.com/pulse/one-startup-i-regret-having-done-10-years-ago-vladislav-solodkiy-td1ke/

[70] https://medium.com/@slavasolodkiy_67243/presentation-of-alexei-navalnys-book-patriot-4991cebe3284

---

[71] https://www.linkedin.com/pulse/private-public-organizations-digital-identity-govtech-solodkiy-jimoe/

[72] https://www.linkedin.com/pulse/ribbit-capital-digital-identity-new-fintech-vladislav-solodkiy-kz15e/

[73] https://medium.com/@slavasolodkiy_67243/ribbit-capitals-new-research-digital-banks-may-be-best-situated-to-become-issuers-of-reusable-b1a229379240

[74] https://medium.com/@slavasolodkiy_67243/the-brain-drain-and-capital-flight-from-russia-would-undermine-putins-regime-cc4735e1950a

[75] https://www.linkedin.com/pulse/complex-saga-arivalbankcom-takeover-vladislav-solodkiy-vznce/

[76] https://www.slideshare.net/slideshow/the-first-fintech-banks-arrival-book-pdf-252-pages-by-vladislav-solodkiy/97363233

[77] https://amzn.to/48AVSyd

[78] https://medium.com/@slavasolodkiy_67243/the-brand-new-fintech-book-recommended-by-wharton-and-insead-f6103bbbc7c7

[79] https://medium.com/@slavasolodkiy_67243/the-future-of-metastates-pragmatic-optimism-and-the-art-of-the-possible-dcb56ea2e7f1

[80] https://www.linkedin.com/pulse/ironic-protagonist-believers-betrayers-vladislav-solodkiy-nyzie/

[81] https://medium.com/@slavasolodkiy_67243/the-predictability-of-r-ts-tactics-the-theater-of-the-arival-s-absurd-45f0690d8376

[82] https://medium.com/@slavasolodkiy_67243/the-regulator-doesnt-care-about-the-truth-there-is-no-perfect-kyc-16385ebbf14d

[83] https://www.linkedin.com/pulse/russian-spy-embedded-world-finance-vladislav-solodkiy-3chie/

[84] https://www.slideshare.net/slideshow/the-russian-spy-embedded-in-the-world-of-embedded-finance/270577210

[85] https://www.linkedin.com/pulse/much-better-thank-your-chief-compliance-officer-

Digital Identity & GovTech:

- "[Digital] Identity is the new money"
- "Ukraine's Next Big Export: Fedorov's DIIA Pioneers Government-as-a-Service Paradigm"
- "Private and public organizations about digital identity, govtech, network states"
- "Ribbit Capital: Digital Identity is the new Fintech"
- "Nansen.ID: Worldcoin for 550 million people in sanctioned countries"
- "How could World ID be better? Or at least useful"

Compliance & Regulatory Challenges:

- "High-Risk Compliance for BaaS and Correspondent Banks"
- "They Are Much Better Than Your Chief Compliance Officer"
- "Compliance Demystified: A Beginner's Guide"
- "The Regulator doesn't care about the 'Truth': there is no perfect KYC"
- "Arrival of the compliance-as-a-service"

Fintech Market and Business Models:

---

vladislav-solodkiy-a2zgc/

[86] https://www.linkedin.com/pulse/three-books-understand-future-being-built-worldcoin-solodkiy/

[87] https://medium.com/@slavasolodkiy_67243/three-events-and-books-to-learn-everything-about-network-states-and-chartered-cities-009b08686c3b

[88] https://www.linkedin.com/pulse/ukraines-next-big-export-fedorovs-diia-pioneers-vladislav-solodkiy-nxuae/

[89] https://www.linkedin.com/pulse/we-useless-class-from-marx-balaji-harari-vladislav-solodkiy-tzbqe/

[90] https://www.linkedin.com/pulse/why-do-you-need-know-griffin-bank-follow-vladislav-solodkiy-kuwbe/

[91] https://medium.com/@slavasolodkiy_67243/wirecards-ghost-has-singapore-learned-its-lesson-69e04f5009be

[92] https://medium.com/@slavasolodkiy_67243/worldcoin-tbd-human-and-their-79-competitors-ae853db998ad

[93] https://www.linkedin.com/pulse/zk-proofs-chasing-problems-dont-exist-vladislav-solodkiy-wqble/

- "Fintech no more: correspondent banking is still an untouched niche"
- "Correspondent banking market overview"
- "Why Do You Need to Know About Griffin Bank and Follow It"
- "Crypto-related clients play cat and mouse with banks"
- "Follow The Money: Brock Pierce, Tether, Deltec, FTX"

Russian Influence & Spy Narratives:

- "From ENRC to Arival: A Pattern of Behavior? Or Just a Coincidence?"
- "Anti-War Russians Face Many Problems, Oligarchs Do Not"
- "The Russian Spy Embedded in the World of Embedded Finance"
- "Jan Marsalek: from Wirecard to Putin's spy"
- "Donald Trump, Russian money & (Anti) Money Laundering"
- "Navalny's Utopia for Realists"
- "The Ironic Protagonist: Believers and Betrayers"
- "Presentation of Alexei Navalny's book "Patriot" & Andrien Brody"
- "Beautiful Russia's Chief Believer"
- "EU on easing the opening of bank accounts for anti-Putins"
- "The Brain Drain and Capital Flight from Russia Would Undermine Putin's Regime"
- "One startup that I regret not having done 10 years ago"

Network States and Charter Cities:

- "From Marx to Balaji: 'Network States' as many 'Dominant Classes' (and no one loses)"
- "Three events (and books) to learn everything about network states and chartered cities"
- "Three books to understand the future being built by Worldcoin"
- "$175 Trillion Problem: Or How to Create the Ultimate Debt Crisis in 12 Easy Steps"
- "We are not the 'useless class'! From Marx to Balaji and Harari"
- "The Future of Metastates: Pragmatic Optimism and the Art of the Possible"

www.ingramcontent.com/pod-product-compliance
Lightning Source LLC
Chambersburg PA
CBHW071523220526
45472CB00003B/1120